CHILD TO PARENT VIOLENCE AND AGGRESSION

Hedwig Verhagen

coramBAAF
adoption · fostering · kinship

Published by
CoramBAAF Adoption and Fostering Academy
41 Brunswick Square
London WC1N 1AZ
www.corambaaf.org.uk

Coram Academy Limited, registered as a company limited by
guarantee in England and Wales number 9697712, part of the
Coram group, charity number 312278

British Library Cataloguing in Publication Data
A catalogue record for this book is available from the British Library

ISBN 978 1 913384 19 7

Project management by Jo Francis, Publications, CoramBAAF
Photograph on cover from www.istockphoto.com
Designed and typeset by Fravashi Aga
Printed in Great Britain by the Lavenham Press
Trade distribution by Turnaround Publisher Services, Unit 3,
Olympia Trading Estate, Coburg Road, London N22 6TZ

For the latest news on CoramBAAF titles and special offers, sign up
to our free publications bulletin at https://corambaaf.org.uk/subscribe.

Contents

Note about the author

Hedwig Verhagen is an independent therapeutic social worker and a social work lecturer at the University of Leeds. After her initial social work training, she completed further training in a variety of therapeutic approaches and gained an MSc in Therapeutic Interventions for Psychological Trauma. She has worked in adoption and special guardianship support services for many years and was part of the small team that set up the Centre for Adoption Support in Warrington. Hedwig has a special interest in attachment, sensory processing and body-focused approaches to working with trauma.

Emma and Will Turner are parents to a birth daughter each from previous marriages and for the last eight years to James, who they adopted when he was three-and-a-half years old. After three years together and realising their parenting journey wasn't yet over, they decided adoption was the way to grow their family. They love to travel and their biggest adventure as a family was eight months of backpacking. James now attends secondary school so they are grounded for the next few years, but still intend to travel when they can.

Daniel Swanson is a pseudonym, as are the other names in his story. Daniel is an American-born 30-something "creative", who lives with his husband and their wonderful adopted son. Three years ago, the Swansons moved to the countryside, where they found space and freedom without the many distractions of the city. They may or may not have two dogs, a cat, five chickens and two canaries when this book is published. Daniel enjoys reading, baking and fossil hunting with his son, gardening, long walks through dragon-infested forests, and any form of creative expression.

The series editor

Hedi Argent is an established author and editor. Her books cover a wide range of placement topics. She has written several guides and story books for young children.

Acknowledgements

Hedwig Verhagen: I would like to thank all the children, young people, adopted adults, parents and carers I have met over the years for sharing their stories, hopes and fears with me. I continue to learn from them each day, and without them this book would not have been written. I would also like to thank my mother, Clara, for always encouraging me, and my sons Emile and Ilya for teaching me about parenting, and for all the joy along the way.

Hedi Argent: I am grateful to all the readers of the manuscript for their helpful comments. I am indebted to Jo Francis of CoramBAAF Publications for her unfailing good humour, patience and support throughout the many years of working together on this series.

Looking behind the label...

Jack has mild learning difficulties and displays some characteristics of ADHD and it is uncertain whether this will increase...

Beth and Mary have diagnoses of global developmental delay...

Abigail's birth mother has a history of substance abuse. There is no clear evidence that Abigail was prenatally exposed to drugs but her new family will have to accept developmental uncertainty...

Jade has some literacy and numeracy difficulties, but has made some improvement with the support of a learning mentor...

Prospective adopters and carers are often faced with having to decide whether they can care for a child with a health need or condition they know little about and have no direct experience of. No easy task...

Will Jack's learning difficulties become more severe?
Will Beth and Mary be able to catch up?
When will it be clear whether or not Abigail has been affected by parental substance misuse?
And will Jade need a learning mentor throughout her school life?

It can be difficult to know where to turn for reliable information. What lies behind the diagnoses and "labels" that many looked after children bring with them? And what will it be like to live with them? How will they benefit from family life?

Parenting Matters is a unique series, "inspired" by the terms used – and the need to "decode" them – in profiles of children needing new permanent families. Each title provides expert knowledge about a particular condition, coupled with facts, figures and guidance presented in a straightforward and accessible style. Each book also describes what it is like to parent an affected child, with either case studies or adopters and foster carers "telling it like it is", sharing their parenting experiences, and offering useful advice. This combination of expert information and first-hand experiences will help readers to gain understanding, and to make informed decisions.

Titles in the series deal with a wide range of health conditions and steer readers to where they can find more information. They offer a sound introduction to the topic under consideration and provide a glimpse of what it would be like to live with an affected child. Most importantly, this series looks behind the label and gives families the confidence to look more closely at a child whom they otherwise might have passed by.

Keep up with all our new books as they are published by signing up to our free publications bulletin at: https://corambaaf.org.uk/subscribe.

Titles in this series include:

- *Parenting a Child with ADHD*
- *Parenting a Child with Dyslexia*
- *Parenting a Child with Mental Health Issues*
- *Parenting a Child affected by Parental Substance Misuse*
- *Parenting a Child with Emotional and Behavioural Difficulties*
- *Parenting a Child with Autism Spectrum Disorder*
- *Parenting a Child with Developmental Delay*
- *Parenting a Child with, or at risk of, Genetic Disorders*
- *Parenting a Child affected by Domestic Violence*
- *Parenting a Child affected by Sexual Abuse*
- *Parenting a Child who has experienced Trauma*
- *Parenting a Child with Toileting Issues*
- *Parenting a Child with Eating and Food Issues*
- *Parenting a Child with Sleep Issues*
- *Parenting a Child with Difficulties in Learning caused by Trauma*
- *Parenting a Child affected by Self-Harm Issues*

Introduction

This is a book about children and young people[1] who sometimes
(or often) express themselves in ways that are experienced as
violent or aggressive by their parents and carers.[2] While this
exploration, together with the case studies in the second part of
the book, may be helpful for any parent living with such challenges,
this book has been written with foster carers, adoptive parents
and kinship carers primarily in mind. This means that child to
parent violence and aggression (CPVA) has been considered in
the context of a child who is growing up separated from their
birth family and who may have experienced abuse, neglect or
other traumas in their earlier years.

---

[1] From now on, I will refer to all children and young people as child/
children.

[2] To avoid unwieldy language, we tend to use the term "parents" to refer
to kinship carers, foster carers and adoptive parents.

I am a therapeutic social worker who specialises in supporting families living with child to parent violence. I have spent my entire social work career working with adoptive and kinship families and I very quickly realised that in order to offer helpful support, I had first to puzzle out why some children express their distress through violent and aggressive behaviours. My first solo duty visit after qualifying as a social worker was related to CPVA. A few weeks after starting my new role in an adoption and special guardianship support team, we received a call from an adoptive parent who said that their 15-year-old child had been arrested after a violent incident at home. It wasn't the first time that a disagreement had resulted in damage to their home, but this was the first time the parent had felt so scared for their own safety that they had phoned the police. The child was now on the way home, and the distraught parent said they were not sure that they would be able to keep themselves and the child safe.

When I arrived at the family's home, I met a child who was furious about having been arrested, didn't want to talk about what had happened, and was even less willing to apologise. The parent said, 'I just don't know what to do', and I must admit I felt very similarly. University had not prepared me to work with children who were violent and aggressive towards adults. Nevertheless, we started talking and somehow, the child and parent were able to come to an agreement about what each of them would do in the future if a discussion started to get heated. The parent agreed to pause and allow the child (and themself) to calm down before continuing the conversation, and the child agreed to leave the room or go for a walk until they felt calmer.

I'd like to be able to say that this was the last violent incident for this family, but sadly, and perhaps predictably, it was not. I soon learned that response to trauma cannot be managed with a contract. It wasn't the last time that the parent phoned the police when things got out of control; over the next few years, the community support officer came to play an important role in the family's life. However, the child did stay at home for the remainder of their teenage years and beyond. Despite the challenges, the relationship between the parent and child remained strong and committed, and when the child (now a young adult) was ready to move out and live independently, they did so with the support of a loving parent. This is what we wish for all children, and especially for children who were unable to grow up in the family they were born into.

Making sense of CPVA

Why did the child act this way? They didn't enjoy it; in fact, they shared with me on several occasions how out of control they felt while these incidents were happening and how scary that was. They described it as being two people: one who was saying horrible things, hitting out and threatening people, while the other was observing and wishing desperately that they could stop and disappear. Sometimes, they were so out of control that afterwards they couldn't even remember what had happened. They told me about the intense feelings of shame, regret and self-loathing that followed these explosive incidents, and how hard it was not to get angry all over again when someone reminded them of what they wished they could forget.

Was this a spoiled child? Did they think that they would get their way with violence and aggression? Did they need a lesson in telling right from wrong? These were some of the suggestions or accusations from relatives, friends and professionals, all trying to be helpful.

The answer is that none of these apply. I believe this child expressed themself through violence and aggression as a result of traumatic experiences in their early years. They had been born to a lone parent who struggled to care for her four young children, due to the impact of poverty, mental health problems and social isolation. Consequently, the children were often unsupervised, hungry, cold and dirty. The child in this case later remembered drinking from the toilet cistern and climbing onto the worktop to look for food in the kitchen cupboard. Their mother's reactions were unpredictable: sometimes loving and playful, but at other times angry or completely unresponsive.

This was the child's introduction to the world: a place where life is tough and you need to look after yourself, because nobody else will. They learned that adults can be loving one moment, and scary the next. When the decision was made that it was too unsafe for the children to remain at home, the sibling group was split up in foster care and eventually adopted by three different families. This child learned at a very early age that the worst can, and indeed does, happen.

What this book covers

This book aims to explore CPVA in a child-centered and trauma-responsive context. I will use a wide definition of trauma as any experience that overwhelms our capacity to respond (Herman, 2022) and shatters our understanding of what we can expect from the world and from ourselves (Janoff-Bulman, 1992). The child-centered approach of this book might at times feel challenging to parents and carers who are living with continued and significant CPVA. However, when discussing strategies, the starting point is always that the child cannot simply decide to stop using aggression and violence, much as they might wish that they could.

We will explore anger in more detail, look at the role of sensory processing (see Glossary) in CPVA, consider identity issues, and how shame and a need to control the environment may all contribute to CPVA. We will look at how CPVA may present in different age groups and explore parenting approaches that may be helpful in the process of encouraging children to develop more positive ways to manage challenges than CPVA.

Please note, all case studies included in Section I of the book are composites, based on author experience.

UNDERSTANDING CPVA

HEDWIG VERHAGEN

What is CPVA?

Over the years, the behaviours that make up CPVA have been described under many different names:

- Parent abuse

- Adolescent to parent violence (APV)

- Battered parent syndrome

- Child and adolescent to parent violence and abuse (CAPVA)

- Child to parent violence (CPV)

In this book, we use the term CPVA, because it captures the wide age range in which this behaviour may occur, as well as the wide range of behaviours. Parents may be reluctant to describe what happens in their home as violence or abuse, and wonder: 'Can a five-year-old really be abusive?' Or they may point out

3

that although they feel they have to "walk on eggshells" to avoid explosive episodes, their child has never actually, physically, hurt them.

It may be helpful to look at some of the definitions used in CPVA research:

> *To dominate, control and coerce members of the family.*
> (Tew and Nixon, 2010)

> *Behaviour is considered to be violent if others in the family feel threatened, intimidated or controlled by it and if they believe that they must adjust their own behaviour to accommodate threats or in anticipation of violence.*
> (Paterson et al, 2002)

These definitions capture the wide range of behaviour that may be described as CPVA. As well as physical and verbal abuse and aggression, it can take the form of bullying, controlling others, destruction of the home and property, verbal and physical threats, and violence towards siblings or pets (Thorley and Coates, 2017). It can be a one-off incident, as well as an ongoing pattern of behaviour. While CPVA may be seen as a form of domestic abuse (violence and abuse from children over 16 is legally classed as domestic abuse), the dynamics are complex and different from violence and abuse perpetrated by a partner. In CPVA, the child is likely to be vulnerable while parents are responsible for their safety and well-being and also understandably reluctant to criminalise their children (Condry and Miles, 2014). In CPVA, both the parent and the child can be victims and in need of safeguarding.

4

How many families are affected by CPVA?

Many parents who are living with CPVA do not know any other families going through similar experiences with their children and therefore believe they must be the only ones. However, CPVA is more common than many people may think. Research suggests that between two and five per cent of families experience CPVA at some point (Gallagher, 2008). This would suggest that in each school class there may be at least one child who has hurt, verbally abused, controlled or coerced a parent or carer. And contrary to some stereotypical views, CPVA has been found to occur all over the world and in all kinds of families. It appears to be unrelated to family composition, socio-economic status, gender or ethnicity of parents or child.

However, CPVA may be more common in families where children have special educational needs, and in adoptive, fostering or kinship families. Up to one-third of adoptive families may have experienced CPVA (Selwyn et al, 2015). Even if a child has not suffered abuse or neglect (common reasons for a child's removal from their birth family), being separated from everything and everyone they have known (including in utero) can be seen as traumatising. And sadly, many children who are adopted or fostered have had multiple experiences of moving homes and of being looked after by different adults. It is therefore imperative to ensure that any discussion of CPVA remains child-centered and non-blaming. While living with a child who expresses themself by using aggression and violence is undoubtedly difficult, distressing, concerning and exhausting for parents, we must remember that there is a reason why the child behaves like this. The impact of CPVA on a child's development will be explored in following chapters, but we will first consider the impact CPVA may have on parents.

CHAPTER **2**

The impact of CPVA on parenting

We learned in the previous chapter that CPVA is more common than people may think. If two to five per cent of families have experienced violence from children, you might imagine that it would be a common topic of conversation amongst parents. Sadly, the perceived stigma and shame attached to having a child who uses violence and aggression stops parents from sharing their concerns. A recent report suggests that many parents only ask for help when they reach crisis point and fear for their physical safety (Brennan *et al,* 2022). This silence prevents people from seeking support for their children and themselves and unintentionally maintains the stigma attached to CPVA. Until there is a greater awareness of the impact and contributing factors, it will remain difficult for parents to share their experiences of CPVA and to seek help.

Why is there a stigma around CPVA?

Society tends to link children's behaviour to their upbringing. Many parents see the ability to influence and control a child's behaviour as a fundamental part of "good parenting"; they worry that they will be seen as "bad" or "weak", if they reveal that their child hurts, verbally abuses or bullies them. Well-meaning advice about maintaining boundaries, staying calm in crises, and modelling appropriate behaviour inadvertently only confirms this fear. People may presume that the behaviour they see or hear has been learned in the child's current family, rather than being a result of early trauma. New parents and carers who have not parented a child before run the risk of others blaming their perceived inexperience as the cause of CPVA.

Another reason why parents may be reluctant to talk about CPVA is their desire to protect their child's reputation. They do not want their child to be seen as violent or aggressive. Parents of children growing up away from their birth families may have an even greater desire to protect their children. Parents may be acutely aware of the stereotypical beliefs some friends and relatives can hold about children who are in care or adopted, through comments such as: 'They come from a violent family, what do you expect?', or 'The apple doesn't fall far from the tree'. Parents may therefore choose to keep the challenges in their home a secret.

The fear of intervention by children's services or the police can add to the reluctance to talk about CPVA and to seek support. Parents of teenagers, in particular, may fear that a request for support from the police could result in a criminal record for their child. Accessing social work support can result in further complexities. Since the impact of CPVA on the child is not always immediately evident, families who ask for help may not meet social care criteria, unless they can persuade the local authority that

7

CPVA poses a significant risk to the child themself or to a sibling. The experiences of the kinship carer below illustrate this:

CASE STUDY: kinship carer

My niece (aged 11) joined our family when she was five. From the beginning, she was always very "bossy", telling me what to do and how to do it. As she has got older, and particularly since she has started secondary school, the bossiness has turned into aggression. If she is upset or anxious about something, she will make demands in a very rude and aggressive way. If I tell her 'no', she'll start screaming and call me all kinds of vile names. She also hits me and pushes me around. When I told her school what was happening, they told me to ring children's services. A social worker did come out to speak to us, but at that time there wasn't anything they could offer to help.

Then one evening, during an argument, I tried to get her to go to her room to calm down. There was a scuffle on the stairs, and she banged her shoulder on the handrail, leaving a big bruise. She told someone at school, and they made a safeguarding referral. It went to a child protection conference, and ironically, they decided she was at risk of physical abuse from me! We have a lot more support now, but it doesn't seem right that she had to get hurt before we got it. And being seen as a risk to my child still upsets me each time I think about it.

Situations where the child is both the victim and the perpetrator can pose a challenge to professionals, particularly if they are not familiar with the link between CPVA and early trauma. Thankfully, professional awareness has been growing over the past ten years, mainly due to adoptive parents who have shared their experiences in the media, as well as through adoption-related charities and other organisations.

Asking for help and support

The advice for adoptive parents, foster carers and kinship carers is to be open and honest about CPVA with the professionals supporting the family, including school staff. Many children who use aggression and violence at home never act the same way at school, or anywhere else outside the home. If a child gets hurt (as in the case study above), school staff will still need to safeguard the child by making a referral to children's services, but knowing the context in which incidents have occurred can make this a less distressing experience for all involved.

Sharing information with other professionals, such as the family's GP and adoption and kinship support agencies, might result in additional support, funding for therapeutic services, or peer support (depending on individual circumstances). It is especially important to inform relevant professionals if parents find they need to use restraining techniques in an attempt to keep themselves and their child safe. These techniques are very difficult to use safely in a home environment and without regular supervision. They are likely to be experienced as traumatic by the child, and carry a significant risk of injury. It is precisely because of these risks that professionals need to know if CPVA has made the situation at home so dangerous that parents feel they have no other option than to restrain their child. This is a very serious signal that additional support is needed without delay.

In an ideal world, responding to and supporting a child when there is CPVA would be considered in the same light as other challenging parenting tasks, such as managing sleep disturbances,

SECTION I

potty training and making sense of the changes that come with the teenage years. Imagine how helpful it would be if a parent could say, 'My seven-year-old bites me when I tell them "no"', and be met with understanding and stories of how others have dealt with similar situations.

The following chapters will explore the different ways in which a child's early traumatic experiences may be related to CPVA, and will suggest a number of strategies for families living with CPVA.

CHAPTER 3

CPVA as a survival response

What are survival responses?

When our brain detects a threat, it offers us a limited range of actions, or "survival" behaviours. The two best known of these are **fight** or **flight**, but research also recognises **freeze**, **friend** and **flock**.

Flocking

We see **"flocking" behaviours** in animals such as sheep, fish and certain kinds of birds. "Flocking together" or "safety in numbers" means that the burden of protection from predators and other survival tasks such as identifying food sources are shared. In humans, flocking as a survival instinct may explain why adolescents tend to group together as they start to explore the world without parental guidance, and how huge football crowds can co-ordinate their chants and gestures.

Friending

"**Friending**" describes a survival response (see Glossary) that is aimed at disarming the source of threat by ingratiating behaviour. Some children who have experienced early abuse or neglect may act in an extremely friendly and compliant way towards new or even seemingly scary adults, in an unconscious attempt to ensure that they won't be hurt. An extreme friending response can even present as sexualised behaviour. This tends to happen if a child has learned through observation, or personal experience, that adults are nice to them when they behave in this way.

Freezing

The "**freeze**" **response** is sometimes also referred to as disassociation. It is triggered when the brain perceives a threat as inescapable and releases chemicals to numb the nervous system in preparation for an attack. For some children this is an immediate reaction to a challenge or stressful situation, while for others it is a survival response when, for instance, fighting or friending have not been successful.

Flight

Children who react to a perceived threat with the "**flight**" **response** may physically run away, but might also hide (for example, under the table, or behind crossed arms), or do whatever they can to avoid the threat, including distraction and procrastination. You may find that a child who has had adverse early experiences will start to talk about anything else whenever the conversation gets close to painful or scary memories. This can be frustrating for parents or professionals if they feel that the child would benefit from talking about their history. However, distraction may be an unconscious survival response to the challenge of reliving traumatic experiences.

Fight

The "**fight**" **reaction** is, as its name suggests, a survival response aimed at defending against a perceived threat with physical force. As in all survival responses, chemicals are released to ready the brain and body for any kind of action needed, whether it is verbal aggression or hitting out. In the fight response, the brain becomes highly focused on the threat; breath and heart rates increase and blood is redirected from the organs to the large muscle groups, to make the body and brain ready for the exertion of a physical response. Because survival responses are a full body and brain experience, children cannot easily think rationally when they are in these states, or simply "snap out of it" when told to stop or calm down. It takes a considerable time before the chemical balance in the body and brain can return to normal after a survival response has been triggered.

Recognising survival responses

Unfortunately, not all survival responses are easily recognised by the child or the adults around them. For example, friending behaviour can be misinterpreted by adults as politeness or as a sign of mature social skills. And children in the middle of a freeze response are often accused of not listening, or of not taking the situation seriously enough. Some children will freeze with a smile on their face, which tends to confuse or perhaps even anger the adults, who may feel that the situation is no laughing matter.

We cannot control which survival response is activated when the brain perceives a threat to our safety, but some are regarded as more socially acceptable than others. When a child is visibly frightened, or seems shy, it is easy to feel empathy for them and to think of ways to help them. But in the case of CPVA, children may be in the middle of a "fight" response and be just as frightened as the child who responds by hiding under a table.

Sadly, because aggression and violence can make carers and adopters and their families feel threatened too, these children are more likely to be seen as badly behaved, unreasonable or selfish than as needing help. When there is CPVA, the parents' own survival responses may be activated, which means that they too may struggle to think rationally.

All humans respond to threat, but if people have experienced trauma, their response is triggered more rapidly. Most of us tend to intuitively understand that a war veteran may have a powerful reaction to sudden, loud noises, which are reminiscent of battlefield sounds. It is perhaps more difficult to understand why a child who experienced early trauma kicks you in response to being asked to turn off an electronic device. Yet the two responses could be seen as very similar. By interpreting CPVA as a trauma and survival response, rather than a character flaw or behavioural problem, we can avoid judging the child unnecessarily, or taking the behaviours personally. This may make it easier to pave the way to a more sensitive and trauma-informed parenting approach.

Therefore, the strategies discussed in this book all stem from the following principles:

- The child is not able to stop using violence and aggression by choice.

- CPVA is too complex to be addressed by simple or "quick fix" strategies.

- As this is a developmental issue, parenting approaches and strategies will need to be continually adapted to the child's age and stage of development.

CHAPTER 4

CPVA and control

From the moment babies are born, they look to their parent/s for connection, nurture (see Glossary) and safety. Babies are so primed to look for human faces that they will, for example, show significantly more interest in cot mobiles with patterns that resemble facial features than those with random shapes (Reid *et al*, 2017). The first time they smile at their parent and the parent smiles back, they sense the delight of reciprocal joy. When the parent works out whether their cry means that they are hungry or need a nappy change, and then feeds or changes them accordingly, the baby experiences that, small and helpless as they are, they can influence an adult's behaviour. Each time the parent meets one of the baby's needs (food, nurture, protection, stimulation), the baby's beliefs in the parent as trustworthy and in themselves as someone who is worth looking after, are reinforced.

As Dan Hughes, a psychologist and psychotherapist, has said, a baby learns who they are through the eyes of others (Hughes, 2007).

When the baby looks into the eyes of a loving, caring parent every day, a parent who provides everything they need to grow and to be at ease, the baby learns that they are loveable and, ultimately, that the world is a safe and predictable place.

However, if parents are not able to do all the things their baby needs, or if the eyes the baby looks into are often vacant, or even hostile, then they are likely to form a very different view of themselves, their parents and the world around them. If they do not have the opportunity to learn to trust in their ability to influence others and in others' willingness to look after them, they may struggle to depend on others. Without the instinctive belief that parents will look after them willingly, a child may feel that they need to manipulate their parents to meet their needs.

The impact of separation

Children who are adopted, or who live with foster or kinship carers, have all been separated from their birth parent/s. Being taken from the birth family home is in itself an experience of powerlessness. Decisions about the child's well-being are made in court rooms and social care offices; sadly, few children, even if they are old enough, have a say in where they will live, once it has been decided that their home is not safe enough.

The reasons for this decision tend to be complex and multi-faceted; however, many children living in kinship, foster or adoptive families have experienced chaotic and dangerous family environments in their first homes, as well as unpredictable and possibly frightening parenting. The younger the child is when subjected to adverse circumstances, the more impact it may have on their sense of safety, because an infant is completely dependent on their parent/s or carer/s for survival, while an older child might have more chance to find food, shelter and nurture elsewhere: perhaps at school, with extended family or neighbours.

When a child who has experienced the hurt of powerlessness settles into a safe home with reliable, nurturing parents or carers, the impact of their earlier experiences does not automatically disappear. They may struggle to trust parental figures to have their best interests at heart, to keep them safe or to give them everything they need to survive. They may lack belief in the possibility of a safe, reciprocal relationship with new adults; or struggle to trust that they will be able to influence these parents, and that it is safe to be influenced by them.

For some children, CPVA is therefore an unconscious strategy to ensure their parents' "obedience". As long as parents do what the child wants, the child feels safe and cared for. But if parents are not obedient, the child may intuitively feel that they do not care about them and will not look after them. In daily life, this may look like a child telling a parent exactly what to do and how to do it. It could be a teenager telling a parent not to look at or speak to them in public, or a toddler's insistence on using a certain cup at breakfast. If the parent veers from these instructions, the child may experience a strong sense of rejection and abandonment, triggering painful memories from their past, and react as if they were once again in that dangerous situation: 'You don't care, you hate me, you never let me have anything, you are the worst parent in the world'.

A sense of control provides safety

Some children's need to control their environment comes from a need to create a sense of predictability in a world that feels chaotic. This need for control may be easier to understand when we consider how many of us use control to feel safe: imagine you are going on a trip abroad, and leaving your house unattended

17

for a while. Would you double-check that you have locked the doors, just to make sure? And how many times would you check that you have your passport with you, on the way to the airport? If we were acting in a purely rational manner, we would put the passport in our bag, lock the doors, and have no further need to check. But in a situation that makes us slightly more anxious than usual, it gives us a dose of comfort each time we have reassurance that the world is as we expect it to be.

When a child has experienced chaotic home conditions, neglect or abuse; if they have witnessed domestic abuse; if they have been taken from one home and expected to settle into another, perhaps repeatedly, then they may continue to have an unconscious foreboding that anything could happen at any time. But if, even for only a few moments, they can make the world look like the picture they have in their head, then their world may feel more predictable.

Children tend to have very little control over where they go or what happens. In order to achieve the relief of being in control, the child needs to somehow make the parent do what they want them to do. And if they lack the belief that they can influence their parents through reciprocal means, they may feel that they have to "fight" their parent to make them obey. So the toddler who has a meltdown when their parent does not give them the "right" cup at breakfast time, and the teenager who puts their fist through a door because their parent won't give them money, may not just be testing the boundaries, but may actually be looking for reassurance that the world is a safe place when life feels very threatening. And when the "fight" survival response is triggered, it may lead to CPVA. The child is convinced, in that moment, that they are genuinely fighting for their life.

Parenting strategies

A note on "strategies": It is understandable that parents in a difficult family situation are keen to find lots of strategies in a book such as this. However, it is worth thinking more closely about what we actually mean by strategies. The dictionary definition of a strategy is 'a plan of action designed to achieve a long-term or overall aim'. This suggests that if you follow a certain strategy, you are planning to act differently than you would have done without that strategy.

We could think of relationships as a dance between two or more people; a dance that is sometimes effortlessly co-ordinated and can at other times be stilted and out of step. A strategy from a parenting book might then be seen as a new dance step introduced by a dance instructor. At first the new step will be a bit clumsy, but if you keep practising, it might become like second nature and can then be incorporated smoothly into your other moves.

Some dance steps just don't feel right though, no matter how hard you practice. You might admire others dancing the tango or the waltz, but it doesn't feel right when you do it. Some strategies are like that too. They may work beautifully for others, but don't feel right for you. If that is the case with any suggested strategy in this book, please feel free to adapt it, or alternatively, ignore it, and try another one that feels more suitable for you and your family.

Perhaps the most helpful approach is to consider the thought underpinning the strategy. What are the drivers behind the behaviour and what is the long-term aim of the strategy? It is this understanding that will enable you to trust your intuition when working out how to respond to situations, rather than being dependent on other people's strategies. With this in mind, the "strategy" parts of this book should be read as suggestions or examples, rather than instructions.

Helping children feel safe

How can parents help their children to feel safe? A loving, effective parent needs to set boundaries, so complying with the child's "demands" at all times is not a good option. What children really need are repeated experiences of their world as a safe, predictable place, and of their parents as trustworthy and dependable adults.

Parents who have got used to "walking on eggshells" may develop a permissive kind of parenting style: they may check all family plans and arrangements with the child to avoid surprises and may allow the child to make or change decisions. This kind of parenting, to avoid CPVA incidents, may inadvertently also create the impression that the child has the ultimate say over what happens, and how the family is run. This is a huge responsibility and at times even too much for an adult to bear, let alone a troubled child or teenager. What is more helpful is to create a safe, predictable family environment where children's opinions are heard and respected, but where parents take clear responsibility for the whole family's safety and well-being.

The strategies below are aimed at allowing parents to take, or to take back, control in an empathic, but authoritative manner. The Non-Violent Resistance (NVR) (see Glossary) parenting approach refers to this as "parental presence". NVR has proved helpful to many families living with CPVA.

Non-Violent Resistance (NVR) aims to help parents and carers address violent and destructive behaviour in children and adolescents using particular strategies that have roots in the civil rights movement.

Being a "good parent"

One explicit way to (re)claim parental authority is for parents and carers to speak about themselves as "a good" mum/dad/ foster carer/aunt/granddad/etc. This works particularly well with younger children: 'I know that you want to keep watching TV, but I'm a good dad and good dads make sure that their children get enough sleep'. This may feel a bit strange at first, but the strategy can be very helpful for children who have experienced parenting that was not good enough in their birth family. It helps them to learn what "good enough" parenting actually looks like, and also provides regular reassurance that their parents not only know how to be a good parent, but are also demonstrating it by their behaviour. Talking about parenting decisions being made because "that's what good parenting looks like", rather than being a whim or personal preference, may also limit triggers for aggression.

This strategy may be especially helpful for parents who have been seriously challenged for a significant length of time, and who may not feel that they are particularly "good" parents. If you are beginning to doubt yourself and to be critical about your parenting skills, it can then be powerful to refer to yourself as a good parent out loud. At first it may sound fake, but in time it will start to feel true.

Clear information about roles

Another strategy for creating safety and predictability for a child who has a strong need to control is to give clear and specific information about child and parent roles and responsibilities.

Children who have experienced neglectful or abusive parenting, or have had multiple changes in care, may not have had the opportunity to learn what to expect from a good parent, and may therefore feel that they alone are responsible for keeping themselves (and possibly others) safe.

An example of this would be a child who wants to check that all doors and windows are locked at night and becomes distressed if they are not allowed to do this, or if the parent doesn't follow the child's "rules" by leaving a window open on a warm evening. When faced with this behaviour, the first step is to reflect on the feelings behind the need. Has this child experienced threats or danger connected to people entering the home unexpectedly, or developed an unconscious association between open windows and doors and danger? It may be tempting to give the child responsibility for checking the doors and windows at night, because this is what they are asking for. However, this may reinforce the feeling that they need to keep themselves and others safe. It would be more helpful to stress the parents' ability to keep the home and everyone in it safe, and to explain that managing the doors and windows is an adult's job. This explanation and reassurance may need to be repeated many times and with great empathy for the feelings behind the child's urge to take control.

Key messages

- A child's need to control is a need for safety.

- Create clarity about adults' and children's roles and responsibilities.

- Talk about yourself as a "good parent/foster carer/aunt/ granddad/etc".

22

CHAPTER **5**

CPVA and emotional immaturity

As we have seen in previous chapters, the changes and unpredictability of some children's early years can continue to have an impact as they grow up. In this chapter, we look at emotional immaturity as another possible consequence.

Emotional maturity

Emotional maturity is the ability to regulate emotions and to express them in a way that is relevant to the situation. Children develop emotional maturity through watching others respond to situations in regulated and proportionate ways. Children who have lived in chaotic, abusive or neglectful environments, or who have had many different caregivers, have had far fewer opportunities to see emotional maturity in action than children who grow up in "'good enough" homes. They are also likely to have missed out on being guided by warm, attentive adults to respond in an

23

appropriate way to challenging, surprising or scary circumstances. For a baby, this might look like being calmly rocked when waking up crying in the night and hearing a whispered, 'There, there, I'm here'. For a toddler, it might be someone to help them up when they have fallen over and to kiss a hurt knee better. For a teenager, it may be an empathic adult who can listen to a story about a friend's betrayal without becoming angry themselves.

Emotional immaturity

Lack of impulse control

When a child has missed out on this kind of modelling (see Glossary) and interaction, they may appear to be a lot younger emotionally than their chronological age. One of the ways in which this immaturity shows is by a lack of impulse control. Nobody is surprised if a toddler gets angry or distressed when someone tells them 'No', or when they are unable to do what they're trying to do. But when a 7, 11 or 15-year-old shows the same toddler-like behaviour, we do not immediately attribute it to emotional immaturity. This presents a double problem for the child: not only do they have to deal with situations that require emotional skills beyond their capacity, but they are at the same time judged for not having those skills. For example, an emotionally immature 10-year-old child at school might regularly misinterpret certain social cues and feel confused, rejected or ridiculed. They might be made angry by comments or in situations that would only mildly annoy others. If they respond to perceived attacks with aggression, and perhaps even violence, both peers and adults will probably disapprove, because 'They should know better at their age'.

Difficulty identifying emotions

Children who are emotionally immature often have difficulty in identifying and understanding their own and other people's emotions. I have met many children and young people who have issues with CPVA, who only recognise "happy" or "angry". All the other emotions are often classified as either being "tired" or "bored". Human beings of all ages have complex emotional lives and to reduce this complexity to good, bad and indifferent means that a great deal of nuance is lost. This may lead a child to misinterpret feelings such as apprehension, disappointment, anxiety or even excitement as a threat, and cause a defensive or attacking reaction. Similarly, children might interpret other people's emotions in this very limited way. Children might ask: 'Why are you angry?' when a parent is concentrating on a task, or simply a bit tired.

Such confusion can contribute to CPVA incidents. The child's nervous system might interpret innocent parental interactions or requests as aggressive demands or threats. I saw an example of this in a family where CPVA tended to happen before school in the morning. After we unpicked the family's routine in a very detailed way, the young person was able to share that when their parents shouted, 'Breakfast is ready' up the stairs in the morning, it made them feel as if what the parents were really shouting was, 'You are late again, and I am furious with you'. This triggered a threat response, sending the child downstairs prepared for a fight. This child had spent their early years with a birth parent who had severe mental health problems and whose responses were often unpredictable. It was no wonder that their nervous system was poised to detect and survive potentially dangerous situations, even though they were now in a safe place.

Unfortunately, not all CPVA incidents have such a clear connection between cause and effect. Clinical psychologist Dan Hughes, who developed the parenting approach PACE and the therapeutic approach Dyadic Developmental Psychotherapy (DDP), encourages us always to wonder about the message behind violent and aggressive behaviour. He suggests that

25

powerful emotions such as anger, resistance and opposition may provide a cover for more vulnerable emotions like sadness, fear and feelings of rejection. This concept was rather poetically described as 'anger being the bodyguard of sadness' by an adopted adult on social media.

Anger as survival mechanism

For many children who are adopted, or who live in foster or kinship care, feeling vulnerable is too risky. Their early experiences have taught them that they need to always be ready to protect themselves. Anger, instead of other, more difficult emotions, becomes an effective survival mechanism. Anger is powerful; it makes people take notice of you and often makes them change their behaviour. Children who have developed this survival behaviour may seem to be chronically angry or disgruntled, which can be exhausting for both child and family. Because they are continually close to "breaking point", any slightly negative experience might become the final straw. This can lead to the "walking on eggshells" situation that so many parents living with CPVA share.

Simply gaining their parents' attention can feel like a survival need for children who have experienced neglect, or who were looked after by a series of carers who were not quite attuned to their needs. They may have learned that aggression and violence are guaranteed to elicit a response from adults, and they may automatically retreat to such behaviours whenever they feel unnoticed, forgotten or ignored. Extreme examples include children throwing things, or becoming verbally abusive to parents who are carrying out necessary daily life tasks, like preparing meals, putting away groceries or taking a shower. These children may feel that their parents will never notice them unless they act aggressively or violently, because they learned early on that this was the only way to get adults' attention.

When considering emotional immaturity, we need to remember that this is a developmental issue, rather than a chronic condition. When a child spends time with emotionally mature and attentive adults, they can gradually start to catch up with the modelling and learning opportunities they have missed. This means that for some children, CPVA can be a developmental stage, which they can grow out of with the help of their parents and other important adults, just like toddlers eventually grow out of the "terrible twos". Anecdotal evidence suggests that some children who express themselves through CPVA during the early stages of joining a new family are able to learn how to respond differently once they have had a chance to build trusting relationships with their parents or carers.

Parenting strategies

Think toddler

If children are younger emotionally than their chronological age, it can be helpful to "think toddler" rather than think that 'They are too old to behave like this'. It may be more useful to wonder 'What does this response tell me about my child's level of emotional skills at this moment?' Emotional skills can be affected by a wide variety of circumstances: tiredness, hunger, feeling safe in a particular environment, or the presence of internal or external triggers for traumatic memories. A child may appear emotionally mature when they are feeling safe and secure, but struggle to access those skills under more challenging circumstances.

A good starting point in such situations is to think what you would do if the child was a toddler. If a toddler responded with anger or aggression, would you try to reason with them, or tell them to calm down? Probably not. You would more likely focus on staying close and reducing stimuli, perhaps through

27

removing them gently to a quieter or more private place, and helping them to calm. If you were taking a toddler into a new situation, you would prepare them for the occasion beforehand, keep them close, explain what was happening and (temporarily) remove them from the situation when you notice the first signs of stress. Distraction might be another strategy to help calm an overwhelmed toddler. Focusing on something completely different may offer an "exit strategy" to a child in the middle of a CPVA incident. This might be pointing out that the cat is doing something funny, or wondering what you might watch on TV later. It may be the arrival of a different adult (an adult or older child in the family, a neighbour or other understanding supporter) that changes the focus of the situation. To be clear, I am not suggesting here that you limit your 8, 11 or 17-year-old child to toddler-friendly activities or environments. I am, however, encouraging you to consider how "thinking toddler" might inform your parenting decisions.

Modelling

If a child has lacked opportunities to witness emotional maturity in their earlier years, it can be very helpful if their adopters or carers are explicit about their own emotional responses in order to offer accessible modelling opportunities. Simply put, when you are having a good time, be sure to let your child know, as they may struggle to interpret non-verbal signals: 'I am having so much fun with you', or 'I am enjoying driving you to school this morning, it's nice to have this time together'. When you are experiencing more difficult emotions, development-appropriate explanations are even more important: 'I probably look a bit grumpy, because I was looking forward to going to the beach today. Now it's raining, I have to think of another plan. I will soon cheer up and think of something else to do', or 'I am annoyed the car has a flat tyre. It's nobody's fault and we can easily fix it, but I am feeling quite frustrated at the moment'. This kind of modelling may also offer opportunities to show how to make yourself feel better, for example, by taking deep breaths, asking for a hug or taking a break for a few minutes.

This strategy not only models how to manage a wide range of emotions, but also that there are no "good" or "bad" emotions, only ones we enjoy feeling and those that are harder to experience. This can be especially powerful in the case of emotions that make the child feel vulnerable, such as shame, disappointment or fear. Children who express themselves through CPVA can benefit from seeing that adults experience the same feelings, but that this does not diminish their strength or power in the long term.

Of course, it is not realistic to expect parents to be in control of their own emotions at all times – especially if families are living with CPVA. Tempers may get frayed, causing the adults to do or say things that they might later regret. It is important to apply self-compassion and to remind yourself that you are a human being with a full range of emotions and an unconsciously triggered threat response, just like your child. Paradoxically, these situations may offer another kind of learning and modelling opportunity after everyone has calmed down: 'I am sorry I shouted at you this afternoon. That must have been scary for you. I don't like shouting and I know you don't like it either. I will do my best to stay calm next time we have an argument.' Learning that everyone makes mistakes and that we can learn from those mistakes can be a powerful message of hope for a child who is struggling to develop emotional maturity.

Children may interpret shouting or powerful body language as aggressive or threatening, and may say during or after an incident that 'You were going to hit me', or 'You are always shouting'. As hard as it is not to respond defensively, particularly if the child has been verbally or physically aggressive, it is much more effective to say, 'I can see that it scares you when I shout/raise my hand. That's

SECTION I

not helpful and I am sorry it happened.' This models offering comfort while revealing vulnerability and self-reflection, and may help the child to think about their own responses in a more reflective way in the future.

Calming down

When the child has fully calmed after CPVA incidents, try to puzzle out together what their experience of the situation was. You may remember and wonder out loud about a particular trigger point: 'I noticed that you got very upset when I said it was time to come off your phone. I wonder what you thought when I said that.' If it is too difficult for a child or young person to answer, you might have to help them by offering suggestions: 'I wonder whether you might have thought that I didn't care that you were in the middle of something? Am I close, or were you thinking something completely different?' If this leads to any understanding of how your child interpreted your interaction, it is important not to jump to defend yourself or to reiterate the rules; that can all wait until later. Before you get to that stage, make sure your child knows that you are trying to understand their point of view: 'So when I say it's time to put your phone away, you think I just want to be mean. That must be hard. If I thought that someone was being mean to me for no reason, I might get angry too.' This kind of conversation helps your child to make sense of their own responses, to learn different ways of looking at a situation and to know that their parent is interested in them, and values them, even after incidents of CPVA.

Identifying emotions

As well as modelling emotional maturity, it is important to help your child to identify their own emotions. Encourage your child to expand their emotional vocabulary and perception, according to their age and level of understanding. This will be easier if you start with the more pleasant emotions: 'I can see on your face that you are enjoying this movie. Are you feeling relaxed, interested, or pleased?' Over time, this strategy can be expanded to the more difficult emotions: 'I can see that you are unhappy about football practice being cancelled. I am sad about it too. How would you describe what you are feeling? Disappointed, annoyed, or resentful?'

When supporting emotional literacy development, it is important to accept whichever way the child chooses to describe their feelings. If we tell children that they are not really feeling what they tell us, we can cause further confusion. For example, if a child says they are scared, but you want to encourage them to go ahead anyway, rather than saying, 'You're not really scared, are you? You've done this lots of times before', it would be more helpful to say, 'Being scared doesn't feel nice, does it? Are you worried, anxious, or terrified?', followed by, 'I am right here. Let's think about what would make this feel a bit safer.'

Accepting a child's emotions can be hard, especially if their emotions feel like a personal attack on you. For example, a child may say that they destroyed their belongings because 'You never let me have anything' or say they don't want you to teach them to ride a bicycle because 'You will drop me'. However, for a child who often expresses themself through CPVA, such reactions may actually represent a genuine breakthrough. Instead of fighting you because they cannot trust that you will keep them safe, they are taking the risk of being vulnerable and telling you how they feel.

As hard as it may be, it is very important not to take negative feelings personally. Living with a child who is emotionally immature and who cannot trust you is demanding, and their parents and carers need a supportive network to help them to deal with their own feelings.

Key messages

- Children who experienced early trauma may be emotionally significantly younger than their chronological age.

- CPVA may be the result of a child's lack of emotional skills to deal with certain situations.

- Anger may hide other more painful emotions, such as fear, sadness and shame.

- At times when CPVA threatens, try to think of what you would focus on, if your child were a toddler.

- Show your child what emotionally mature responses look like by your own behaviour.

- Focus on understanding emotions before looking for solutions.

CHAPTER 6

CPVA and shame

In this chapter, we explore shame as a possible contributing factor to CPVA. Although nobody enjoys the hot, dizzying or nauseating feeling when we are caught doing something wrong, or realise that we have made a mistake, guilt and shame are necessary human emotions. Despite the discomfort of shame and guilt, we need these feelings to guide our behaviour, learn from experience and feel empathy for others.

Guilt and shame

The difference between guilt and shame is that guilt makes us feel 'I have *done* something wrong', while the impact of shame is 'I *am* someone wrong'. Guilt occurs when we realise that we have made an error of judgement, or that our behaviour has (unintentionally) had a negative consequence. This focus on behaviour motivates us to make changes. Therefore, after the initial pain or discomfort of guilt, we tend to experience more constructive feelings, such as a sense of responsibility and a belief in our ability to make amends.

In contrast, shame is focused on the kind of person we are, and what the shame-inducing incident has revealed about us. Shame feels like a spotlight on all our imperfections, exposing the worst about us to scrutiny. This intense focus on the self means that there is less space for empathy for others. Shame makes people feel that they can't change and are doomed to repeat the same mistakes. Consequently, shame does not prompt the same commitment to change as guilt does.

When a parent corrects a child after breaking a rule or making a mistake, it creates an unpleasant feeling of guilt for the child. If the parent then reconnects with the child and shows them that they are still loved, the unpleasant feeling dissipates. For example, a toddler puts their hand near an electricity socket. The parent moves their hand away and says 'No, that's dangerous', followed by a smile. Minutes later the child puts their hand in a plant pot, ready to take a mouthful of earth. Again, the parent moves them away, this time making a face and saying 'Yuk', and then shows the child a toy to distract them, smiles and says, 'Look at this'. This correction–guilt–reconnection process might take only a few seconds and will be repeated thousands of times in the first few years of a child's life. Over time, this helps the child to trust that correction is followed by connection, which means that making mistakes or making an unwise choice will not feel like the end of the relationship, but more like part of a positive learning process.

Children who are adopted or who live with foster or kinship carers have often missed out on this kind of sensitive parenting during their earliest years. They may have lived in neglectful environments without appropriate parental supervision. Without supervision, very young children will inevitably get into trouble.

34

Managing the consequences of their actions without support can be overwhelming. Imagine a toddler left unsupervised in their cot for an extended period of time. To manage the boredom, they might climb out of the cot and hurt themselves, or end up exploring the contents of their nappy. Parents who haven't got the capacity to see situations from their child's perspective might then tell the child off harshly, or even aggressively, when something goes wrong, or when the child's needs inconvenience them. If repeatedly reprimanded and without reconnection afterwards, the child is left with the horrible feeling that their actions result in pain, upset and chaos. They may then internalise this feeling and see themselves as bad, dirty and unworthy. Over time, the child will learn to believe that there is something badly wrong with them, and that they are just not good enough to be loved and to succeed; they will then be left feeling shamed, rejected and alone.

Responses to shame

Experts suggest that there are three responses to shame, which are all an unconscious effort to avoid, or disconnect from, the discomfort of shame (Hartling *et al*, 2000). These three responses are:

- a move towards;
- a move away;
- a move against.

The "**move towards**" is aimed at trying to appease and please others. Let's imagine a scenario where a child accidentally knocks a glass of water off the table, shattering the glass. A "move towards" response would involve profuse apologies, perhaps more than would seem necessary. Following the incident, the

35

child may go out of their way to be "good" and to seek lots of reassurance that you still care for them. The "**moving away**" response describes behaviours focused on trying to avoid shame through hiding, withdrawing, silence and secrecy. In the spilt water scenario, that might be an attempt to cover up what happened by anxiously trying to mop up the water and hiding the shards of glass before anyone notices. The child may leave the room without telling anyone what happened, or hide away in their own room, refusing to speak to anyone.

While we might all display different shame responses at different times, many people unconsciously gravitate towards one type of shame response more frequently than to others. Children who express their distress through CPVA are likely to react to experiencing shame with "**move against**" responses. The aim of "move against" responses is to try to escape the pain of shame by gaining control over others through humiliation or aggression. This may include physical or verbal aggression and attacks: 'I hate this ugly glass and I hate you too'. It may involve bullying or threats: 'What are you going to do, cry again?', or 'Who cares about a stupid glass; next time I'll break your favourite vase'.

It can be difficult for parents and carers to recognise these responses as survival strategies from shame, one of the most helpless emotions humans experience. If a child is overly apologetic, or anxiously hides away, it may be easier to feel empathy for them and to offer a nurturing response: 'I can see that really upset you. Let's have a hug and tidy it up after. Everyone spills things sometimes. Yesterday I knocked over the orange juice, do you remember?' But if, instead, a child responds with verbal and physical aggression and perhaps physical violence, it is much harder to recognise the shame trigger beneath the reaction. The concept of "toxic shame" (see Glossary) may help us to understand this behaviour better.

Toxic shame

If children believe that they are unlovable and not as good as others, making a mistake or being caught breaking the rules (even if unintentionally) can trigger an emotion called "toxic shame" (Hughes, 2017). This term refers to a shame experience that completely overwhelms the nervous system and causes physical symptoms such as feeling hot, dizzy, having a dry mouth, nausea, tingly limbs and a raised heartbeat. Those of us lucky enough not to have experienced significant early life trauma will probably only have had a limited number of experiences of toxic shame in our lifetime. These incidents are usually memorable. When we talk about them, we use language such as 'I wished the ground would have swallowed me up' and 'I didn't know where to look'. If we consider that children who experienced developmental trauma might feel toxic shame several times a day, we can start to understand why they may unconsciously use "move against" strategies to disconnect from that intensely uncomfortable experience.

Parenting strategies

As we have seen above, shame responses are unconscious and immediate. That means that it is very difficult for a child to alter their reactions to shame-inducing situations by using logical reasoning or a 'What could I do differently next time?' approach. The strategies below are therefore predominantly aimed at developing children's awareness of their shame triggers and increasing their shame resilience (see Glossary) through self-reflection and learning about the world, mostly by watching their parents and carers.

Developing "shame resilience"
Experts recommend developing shame resilience to help manage

37

the vulnerability shame can lead to. Elements of shame resilience include empathy, connection, awareness, normalising, and being able to laugh about experiences with a trusted other. Parents can model this kind of resilience by sharing (in an age-appropriate way) their own experiences of shame, their initial response and how they are making sense of it now. For example, a parent may share an embarrassing scenario at the supermarket, when they forgot to scan an item on the self-service machine and were caught out in a random check. They could share their emotional reaction: 'I was so embarrassed, and it felt like everyone in the shop was looking at me'. Their initial response might have been to repeatedly say 'sorry' to the attendant, or perhaps they got cross with them instead. The aim of sharing these kinds of stories is to communicate to the child that everyone experiences the discomfort of shame; that it can make us act in ways that may seem strange or inappropriate afterwards; that we may regret what we said or did; but most importantly, that these feelings don't last forever: 'It doesn't seem such a big deal now, and the woman in the shop has probably forgotten all about it'. The more engaging, and perhaps even funny, the parent can make their story, the better: 'You should have seen my face when I realised I hadn't scanned the bananas! I've never been so surprised by a banana before.' In time, the child may start to feel safe enough to tell their own shame stories and to experience the relief of sharing.

Children whose CPVA may be triggered by shame could benefit from learning that all human personalities are made up of many parts (Schwartz, 2013), and that while one part of them might get angry and aggressive when challenged, they have other parts that are gentle, kind and loveable. The importance of this message is that when the child's "hitting out" part is the most powerful, their "calm" and "gentle" parts are still there; they are just harder to notice.

This kind of perspective may prevent the child from seeing

themself as "all bad" after CPVA incidents. It is not a matter of denying that what happened was not right, but by being curious about their different parts, the child may be able to think about the incident without being overwhelmed with shame. It might also offer opportunities to ponder why certain parts tend to show up at difficult moments. Perhaps their "angry" part kept them safe when life was scary and was necessary for their survival, but it could now take a well-deserved break and let other parts manage difficult situations. These kinds of conversations can offer the child hope that as they mature, and their other parts grow stronger, they will be able to respond to challenges with their calmer parts more often.

Acknowledging success

Another strategy is to explicitly acknowledge a child's success whenever you see them cope with a potentially shame-inducing experience without anger or aggression. Be aware that acknowledging success is not the same as praising a child. Sadly, many children who experience high levels of shame may be triggered into a defensive reaction by enthusiastic praise. Because shame tends to feel like being in the spotlight, anything that makes the child the centre of attention can start to feel too risky. Being put in the spotlight for success by heartfelt praise can therefore also induce an angry, "move against" shame response.

Acknowledging success is more low-key and evidence-based than praise. Instead of saying 'Good job, well done!', you might say, 'It is upsetting when your baby sister snatches your toys. You probably felt quite angry with her, but you just looked for something else to play with. You are a wise and patient brother', or: 'I realise that you must have been disappointed and annoyed when I said I couldn't give you a lift to your friend's house. I am impressed at how quickly you thought of another way to get there. You are such a good problem-solver.' You share what you observe, and let the child know what that reveals about them as a person. This way of recognising success may feel strange and counter-intuitive at first, because you are celebrating the kind of behaviour that you would expect from the child anyway. However, if a child struggles to meet behavioural expectations such as not hurting or scaring others, then calm, patient, wise and mature behaviour is definitely something to celebrate. It may be helpful to keep a record of the times that your child manages a difficult situation without CPVA. This could serve as a helpful reminder during difficult times, and as a reason to hope for both parents and children.

Learning new skills often involves small doses of shame, as we inevitably get things wrong at first. It is this feeling of shame that motivates us to do better next time and to keep working towards mastery. But for a child who frequently experiences "toxic shame", learning through trial and error is likely to be too overwhelming. It may be much easier for them to learn from what is going right, rather than from what is going wrong.[1] 'I saw you sharing those sweets with your brother, that shows what a kind girl you are' may be more effective and much less shame-inducing than 'Don't eat all those sweets, they're for your brother too'. And 'I noticed how patient you were while I was on the phone' may be more effective than, 'Please be quiet when I'm on the phone'. This approach means that parents need to look out for rules being followed, rather than broken. While this is a very different approach to parenting than many parents and carers are used to, it has many potential benefits, for the parent as well as the child. One positive effect of being a "success detective" is that parents become better at noticing how much is going right, even on days with CPVA. Or, as one parent put it: 'I feel that I am allowed to enjoy my child again, no matter how challenging I find their behaviour sometimes'.

---

[1]   This is a Nurtured Heart Approach strategy. More information about this approach can be found at https://nurturedheartinstitute.com.

Learning to cope positively with directions

Children who struggle with shame often also struggle with
parents' directions or advice. This may be one of the reasons
that homework is a frequent trigger for CPVA. To a child with
low self-esteem, parents' well-meaning support might sound
like criticism, or even rejection. It can be helpful if parents can
model coping positively with criticism and advice themselves. For
example, if a child complains about what is for dinner, rather than
reacting defensively, it might be a valuable lesson for the child
to see their parent respond to their grumbles with playfulness:
'I know, roasted cauliflower is nobody's favourite. Wouldn't it be
great if pizza was just as healthy as cauliflower? Then we could eat
it every day.' And if the parent makes a mistake, for example, by
burning the pizza or dropping a cup on the floor, it offers a great
opportunity to show how to deal with a mishap with grace and
humour. And of course, if your child can do the same, it offers a
good opportunity to acknowledge their success.

If your child is in a calm mood, you might share your observation
of times when they experienced shame: 'I have noticed that
you feel bad when you don't know what to do in your maths
homework. I can understand that because there are usually a few
really tricky questions.' This encourages your child's awareness
of their feelings of shame. Giving a child the choice between
'Would you like my advice, or do you need me just to listen to
you?' is also helpful. If parents can offer an empathic ear while
the child expresses their frustrations or difficulties, and resist the
temptation to explain where they have gone wrong and what to
do instead, the child may be able to work out a solution themself,
or be calm enough to ask for help.

Support to make choices

Another strategy to help children manage shame is to support
them to make choices. For children who feel toxic shame, making
any choice can feel like a risky and potentially shame-inducing

challenge. What if their choice turns out to be the wrong one? Or what if they can't cope with the consequences of their choice? However, taking choices away altogether would clearly not support the child's development and could create even more frustration. One way of making choices less risky is to limit them to two explicitly good options: 'Would you like cereal or toast? Both are OK with me.' Or in more complex situations: 'You have two options: going to homework club after school or doing your homework at home. I will support you whichever one you choose.' This will give the child opportunities to learn that making choices can be safe and eventually even fun.

Creating opportunities for fun may be especially helpful for children who experience high levels of shame. As we have seen, the fear of shame can make a child risk-averse. As a consequence, some children who experienced early trauma may come across as very serious or chronically grumpy, choosing to miss out on fun rather than risking humiliation. In order to have fun, we have to allow ourselves to be vulnerable enough to be surprised and perhaps to look and act a bit daft. If children manage feelings of shame with CPVA and have a need to control their environment to feel safe, spontaneous fun may feel sadly out of reach.

Parents can help children to experience the freedom of laughter and "letting go" by modelling it themselves. When we play, we communicate that the world is a safe place – safe enough to stop scanning the environment for threats and to enjoy the moment. This can take the form of an impromptu kitchen disco, enthusiastically joining in with a game, or fully concentrating on a film that the child is likely to enjoy. Enjoyment can be expressed non-verbally through relaxed and playful body language, as well as verbally, by lightness of tone. If a child's experience of shame has made them self-conscious, they may be easily embarrassed by their family's antics, so it might be advisable to confine these moments to the privacy of home or somewhere they are unlikely to bump into people they know. Some families find that their children relax more easily in a playground, swimming pool or park away from their community. If the child shows signs of enjoyment or relaxation, it can be helpful to acknowledge it, to help them notice how enjoyment and relaxation feel.

Helpful adults

Finally, a child who is aggressive and violent towards their parents may benefit by having an adult from outside the family to talk to. When children are adopted, or live in foster or kinship care, the parental relationship can be emotionally challenging and confusing. Their first experiences with parents may not have been positive, or they may struggle with conflicted loyalties. Not only is a positive relationship with an adult outside the family associated with higher levels of resilience, it may also offer opportunities to access an adult perspective on situations that are too shame-inducing to discuss with a parent, or during times when their relationship with parents is too strained for open conversations.

This role can be filled by a professional, such as a social worker or therapist. However, children do know that it is a professional's job to spend time with them and the reality is that professionals may change jobs or that the funding for support comes to an end, resulting in yet another loss.

It would therefore be preferable to develop a connection with an understanding neighbour or friend of the family. This relationship needs to be given time to develop naturally, alongside the adult's explicit messages about their respect for the child and about how much they look forward to the time they spend together. Once a trusting relationship has developed, the adult should let the child know that they are aware that CPVA occurs in their family, and that their concern is for the child's well-being. They might say, for example: 'It must feel horrible to get so upset. I hope you're OK.' This conveys to the child that all their parts are accepted, including the part that expresses itself through CPVA. Once this message has been received, the adult's role could include checking in with the child after CPVA incidents, to help them make sense of what happened and why and, if appropriate, think through actions they might need to take to put things right.

The involvement of a trusted adult is likely to be helpful for the child but can also support parents. As discussed in Chapter 2, living with CPVA may cause parents to feel shame about their parenting, or their family circumstances. Involving supporters can break the culture of secrecy that often affects families living with CPVA. In the same way that the child benefits from being accepted and appreciated just as they are, it can be very powerful for parents and carers to tell their child's supporter about the family's most difficult moments and to find acceptance and support instead of judgement. Adult supporters do need to understand why children who have experienced early trauma and unpredictability may express their distress through CPVA, and they may benefit from reading a book such as this.

Key messages

- Early trauma can cause children to feel "toxic shame", a feeling that there is something wrong with them, which makes them unloveable.
- CPVA can be an unconscious attempt to escape the feeling of shame.
- Encourage shame resilience by showing how to deal with shameful situations positively.
- Teach rules and expectations by noticing when the child is already following them.
- Offer only good choices.
- Consider outside support for your child.

44

CHAPTER 7

CPVA and the body

Over the past 20 years, we have come to an understanding that the mind and body are closely connected. Emotions often start off as bodily sensations, and our body reacts to emotional states (Siegel and Payne Bryson, 2011). For example, butterflies in your stomach might make you realise that you are nervous, and being excited can make you feel energised.

How stress affects the body

As we have seen in previous chapters, early traumatic experiences can affect the way a child responds to stressful situations. Their body might have become accustomed to being in a chronic state of stress and respond to anything out of the ordinary with an unconscious and strong drive to prepare for fight or flight. While this has an impact on emotional states, it can also have an impact on physical health and well-being (van der

Kolk, 2014). The immediate effects include a raised heartbeat, dry mouth and changes in body temperature. Longer term physical reactions to chronic readiness for survival include exhaustion and problems with joints and muscles. Digestion, which requires the body to be in a resting state, is not prioritised when the body is stressed, which may explain why so many children who are adopted or who live in foster or kinship care have difficulties with bowel health, constipation and other digestive issues. This may also help explain why so many children who have experienced developmental trauma struggle with wetting and/or soiling, particularly at times of stress (for more, see Fenton, 2019). Children's immune systems can also be affected by chronic stress, which may leave them more vulnerable to colds and flu.

The physical manifestations of stress mean that a child who has suffered early trauma may experience their body in a different way than someone fortunate enough to have had consistent good care and attention. Bessel van der Kolk, a psychiatrist who has done extensive research into the impact of trauma on the body, coined the phrase "Hurt people hurt people" about adults with post-traumatic stress disorder (PTSD) (see Glossary). This phrase can be equally well applied to the children we are thinking about in this book. Children who express themselves through CPVA physically and emotionally hurt their parents and carers because they themselves have been hurt.

Some children find the surge of energy that accompanies the stress response uncomfortable and unconsciously look for a way to rid themselves of that feeling. They may shout, jump up and down, or dangle upside down on the sofa. They may push their sibling or parent, or might hit out, all because their body is "fizzing" with stress and anxiety. If they are told at such times to calm down, behave or sit properly, they may be left with an uncomfortable feeling. A body made ready for action needs to take action, one way or another.

Some children visibly shake as a result of being in survival mode. Shaking can be our body's natural response to scary and stressful situations. If a child is shaking with emotion, it is advisable to allow them to release anxious energy in this way, rather than to try to stop them from shaking. If the child seems scared or upset by their shaking limbs, gently reassure them that this is a normal response to being very angry, scared or even excited.

Sensory processing

When thinking about CPVA and the body, we also need to consider sensory processing. We are all aware of the five senses: sight, smell, sound, taste and touch. We may be less familiar with the vestibular and proprioceptive senses (see Glossary); the first helps us to move and remain balanced, and the second lets us know where our body is in space. Together, these seven senses help us to interact with the outside world and to understand how we move around in our environments (Lloyd, 2020). Babies start to develop their senses even before they are born. After birth, the senses mature and integrate further every time the baby eats, is carried and explores their world.

If children grow up in neglectful or abusive environments or experience too many changes to feel safe enough to explore their environments, this process tends to happen less smoothly. As a result, their sensory systems may be underdeveloped, and challenge the way they experience their world and bodies. For example, a child who was not carried and rocked enough as a baby may later find movement unsettling and anxiety-provoking. Children who did not have enough opportunities to develop their balance system and core strength may struggle to stay upright, and slope forward when they sit at a table, and lean on walls or other people while walking. If a child's tactile system (see Glossary) is underdeveloped, a light touch may feel uncomfortable or even painful. If a parent brushes the child's hair, or touches their arm, the child may cry out in pain and say,

'You hurt me'. For these children, sensory stimuli can quickly become overwhelming and CPVA may be the result, or some other desperate measure to take control of a situation that feels dangerously out of control.

Some children's sensory processing development has been affected in such a way that their bodies do not register movement, taste or touch very well, which means that they are always craving more sensory input. These children might always seem to be banging and crashing into walls, doors and other people. They may seek very powerful stimuli and might be genuinely confused and surprised when other people complain about their hard, squeezing hugs, forceful pats on the back, or even bites, and may then try to minimise or deny their actions. To them, what others see as CPVA is not violent or aggressive at all; in fact, if others did the same to them, they would welcome it.

Parenting strategies

Start with HALT

When we look at body-focused strategies, it is important to start with the basics. Dan Siegel encourages parents to consider "HALT" whenever their child is dysregulated (see Glossary) (Siegel and Payne Bryson, 2011). HALT stands for Hungry, Angry, Lonely and Tired. The advice is to address these things first, before considering any other strategies. Give the child a snack, connect with them and make sure they get enough sleep or at least an opportunity to rest. Of course, if children express themselves by CPVA, the Angry part may be a little more complicated to address.

Learning what emotions feel like

Many children not only avoid thinking about their anger, but also avoid feeling it in their bodies. It can be very helpful for them to develop a greater awareness of what "angry" feels like, but this can be tricky. It may be easier to start with noticing positive reactions. Parents can model this and encourage the child to join in. For example, they may say: 'I am really looking forward to having an ice cream later. I can already imagine the taste in my mouth and my tummy feels excited even thinking about it. How about you?'. Other examples could be noticing what it feels like to snuggle under a soft blanket or to take a warm shower or bath. Once the child is comfortable with noticing pleasant physical responses, parents can encourage awareness of more difficult experiences, such as disappointment or impatience. The best way to do this is to first focus on shared challenging situations, such as waiting in a queue: 'This seems to be taking a long time. I am getting an impatient feeling in my legs and in my stomach. What does waiting feel like in your body?' If the child can tolerate this, they might also be able to check in with their body when they have an unpleasant experience or feeling. The purpose is to help the child to recognise the fleeting nature of emotions, so that when they notice anger, or another difficult feeling, they unconsciously realise that this too will disappear before too long. Enduring painful feelings is easier if you know that they won't last forever. Furthermore, increased awareness is associated with a greater ability to regulate (van der Kolk, 2014), which means that the child may have a better chance to manage challenging situations without violence or aggression.

Creative strategies

Increased awareness of feelings can be very difficult to achieve. If the mindful approach does not work for your child, they might find it easier to get to know their anger through creative strategies, such as drawing or painting. Encourage your child to explore what their anger would look like if it were a person, animal or fantasy creature. Seeing a picture of their anger can make it feel less intimidating, especially if they can give the anger-creature a funny name, or perhaps a silly hat. Another question to explore might be: what would anger taste like, if it was a food? What might it smell like, and what kind of texture would it have? Would it be a slimy, green dessert, or a bowl of spiky fruit? Once a child can look at their anger without fear and without being overcome with shame or anxiety, it will become easier to think about it too.

If a child can think about their anger, they can start to learn more about it. The first lesson is that anger can get bigger or smaller, depending on how you deal with it. Explore together: what makes it grow bigger, and what might make it shrink? For example, you might puzzle out whether being in a rush or siblings touching their toys can make anger grow. And your child may say that a hug will make anger smaller. If they suggest an inappropriate strategy to shrink anger, for example, hitting their sibling, you can use it as a starting point for a more workable option. Perhaps hitting the mattress might have a similarly calming effect as hitting their sibling? Once a child has become dysregulated (see Glossary), it is usually too late for calming strategies such as punching a cushion or stamping feet. However, if the child is invested in getting to understand their anger, they will be more likely to notice it before it escalates, and be more willing to experiment with regulating strategies.

Regulating strategies and the sensory system

When the fear response is triggered, energy is released into the big muscle groups, to prepare the body to fight in self-defence, or to run away. Regulating strategies can therefore be any activity that offers the body the opportunity to use up that excess "survival" energy, by exercising the thighs, arms or core muscles. Activities could include running, jumping, pushing and pulling. In sensory processing terms, these activities are known as "proprioceptive" strategies, meaning that they help the brain to know the body's position in space, the whereabouts of the different body parts, and how much strength the muscles need to move (Lloyd, 2020). These kinds of activities not only help a child to use up anxious energy, but also have a calming effect on the whole sensory system. The most creative sensory strategies I have come across over the years have included encouraging a small child to carry heavy cookery books from one room to another, pushing against the wall to "make this room a little bigger", and walking home from school via the playground to use up extra energy released during the school day.

If children's sensory systems are easily overstimulated by sounds, smells, textures or movement, none of the strategies listed in previous chapters are likely to reduce the frequency or severity of CPVA outbursts. Over-responsive sensory processing systems can make a child feel unsafe in their own bodies. Understanding the child's sensory system, as well as helping them to understand their own body's responses better, may be helpful. If parents can work out what might be upsetting the child's sensory experience, then significant improvements might be found quite quickly. For example, if a child is over-responsive to bright fluorescent lights, light sensitivity glasses can reduce discomfort and thereby bring down levels of stress. Helping a child to reduce sensory overstimulation can feel like immediate relief, like removing a thorn from a finger. Similarly, offering a child with an under-responsive sensory system the kind of activities that satisfy their sensory needs could help them to feel more alert, present and calm very quickly. They may find that they are more "switched on" after doing a few vigorous star-jumps. While we need to be careful to avoid considering sensory interventions as a panacea for families affected by CPVA, it is worth exploring whether behaviour that looks like violence and aggression might be connected with the way in which the child's nervous system interacts with their environment.

Occupational therapists who specialise in sensory processing might be able to help with assessments and recommendations, as well as therapeutic social workers, psychotherapists and psychologists who have done additional training to support children with under-developed sensory systems. Suggestions for organisations offering this service can be found at the end of this book.

Key messages

- CPVA may be an unconscious survival response to something your child experiences as threatening.

- CPVA may be connected to an under-developed sensory processing system, or sensory processing disorder.

- CPVA may be affected by hunger, lack of sleep, or lack of/too much stimulation.

- Encourage awareness of what anger feels like in the body.

CHAPTER 8

A case study and family support plan

In this final chapter of Section 1, we consider what a possible support package may look like for a child who expresses their distress through CPVA by considering a case study of a child named Jayden. Even though the support needs of each child and their family will be unique, this may give you some ideas about the kind of therapeutic interventions and other support services that may benefit your family.

CASE STUDY

Jayden, now aged 10, moved in with his mums, Magda and Rebecca, when he was nearly three years old, after being looked after in foster care for a little over a year. Magda and Rebecca got on well with Jayden's foster carers during the introductions but were surprised to hear that the couple separated as soon as Jayden's placement ended.

Jayden's birth mother, Stella, was 17 when he was born and had her own social worker as she was regarded as being at risk of child sexual exploitation. Stella never disclosed who Jayden's birth father was. She struggled to prioritise Jayden's needs but often left him with family members, friends or neighbours while she went out. Jayden was taken into foster care following an incident when he was found unsupervised in the flat by neighbours, who were alerted by the sound of the fire alarm going off.

Ever since Jayden joined Magda and Rebecca's family, he has had very intense outbursts, with lots of screaming and hitting out. When he was little, his parents saw this as developmentally appropriate "toddler tantrums". However, as he has got older the outbursts have increased in frequency and intensity, and they are now very concerned about Jayden and their family.

Magda and Rebecca say that seemingly anything can lead to an incident. They can't say 'no' to Jayden without causing an outburst. Rebecca worries that Jayden is starting to use aggression to get his own way, because they have sometimes dropped consequences for rude or violent behaviour, just to keep the peace.

When all is well, Jayden is described as an affectionate boy who enjoys his mums' company, although he would as happily stay on his phone or tablet all day. Having to come off these devices can become a challenge. He also enjoys sports and is a keen rugby player. Getting ready for training or matches is a frequent trigger point and a while ago he was stopped from going to rugby, as a consequence for repeated angry and disrespectful behaviour. The same has happened when days out are planned. Magda and Rebecca know that they'll probably have a good day if they can get to the beach or the woods, but Jayden often gets so dysregulated while getting ready or getting in the car that days out have now become rare.

School staff report that Jayden is a quiet and well-behaved pupil who does not display any aggression. But he is usually in a grumpy mood when Magda picks him up at the end of the day. If anything unexpected then happens, this grumpiness can easily turn into opposition and shouting, or into aggressive and violent incidents.

During incidents, Jayden may kick, bite, scream and throw things. Recently, he almost pushed Rebecca down the stairs during a scuffle, which really frightened his parents. Both Rebecca and Magda feel that they are constantly walking on eggshells around Jayden. Magda says that she is willing to try anything to improve matters. Last year, she and Jayden engaged in a Theraplay (see Glossary) intervention funded by the Adoption Support Fund (see Glossary). While they both enjoyed the sessions, Jayden seemed to become more dysregulated afterwards, and the two or three days after each session were very challenging for all of them. Rebecca says that she has started to avoid spending time with Jayden and that she can't relax until Jayden is in bed. Even when Jayden is calm, Rebecca feels "on edge" around him. She admits that she gets a sick feeling in her stomach each time she hears Jayden raise his voice, even during play.

The support plan

Making sense of CPVA

Jayden lived with his birth mother, Stella, for the first 18 months of his life. During this time, he experienced unpredictable parenting from his young and vulnerable mother. He was cared for by a variety of people. We will never know quite how he experienced this, but we can guess that he would have been unsettled by not knowing who he was going to be with and how they would care for him. It is likely that some of the family members, friends and neighbours may have struggled to settle him. It takes time to become attuned to a baby's needs: to work out whether a cry means hunger, upset, being wet, or feeling poorly. Perhaps Jayden spent a lot of the time feeling scared, hungry and uncomfortable. Because of his early experiences, he may unconsciously fear that whatever is coming next will make him feel unsafe and uncared for. This may be one of the reasons why Jayden now seems to struggle with transitioning from one activity to the next.

Jayden's young life changed completely after an incident when he was left unsupervised in a flat while the fire alarm was going off. We don't know how often he had been left on his own before this, or how long Stella had been gone on this occasion. We can only imagine how he would have experienced the loneliness, the shock of the noisy fire alarm, and suddenly being removed from his home by strangers. He was taken to an unfamiliar foster home, to be cared for by more strangers. It seems safe to presume that this was a traumatic experience, and one that is likely to still affect him. We can only guess how Jayden's nervous system responds now, when he hears a sudden loud noise or is surrounded by unfamiliar adults. It is likely that Jayden is still frequently scared and upset. Perhaps anger has become a way of managing these difficult emotions that make him feel vulnerable?

When Jayden first joined Magda and Rebecca's family, he was

said to have intense outbursts. As he was still very young at the time, his parents thought of these as "toddler tantrums". However, Jayden's screams and hitting out may have been more than toddler tantrums; they may have been an expression of the fear and confusion he felt, especially after moving to yet another unfamiliar home. Perhaps moving again left him feeling that no home will ever be permanent? The fact that these outbursts have increased in frequency and intensity suggests that Jayden might experience high levels of anxiety or feel overwhelmed much of the time. It also suggests that he has not yet been able to manage his intense emotions without aggression and violence.

Jayden's love of sports and outdoor activities suggests that they calm him. Similarly, he may have found that being engrossed in electronic devices helps him to switch off and relax a little. Unfortunately, his difficulties with transitioning from one place or activity to the next impact on both of these calming strategies. He regularly misses out on opportunities to use his anxious energy in a positive manner through physical exercise, because of his aggressive behaviour when he needs to get ready to go out. His difficulty in letting go of the relief that devices bring him also gets him into trouble, which sadly leaves him without a reliable way to calm his anxiety.

Suggested family support

The first priority when supporting this family would be to help Rebecca and Magda to understand and empathise with Jayden's experience of the world. As family life moves on and new challenges arise, it is easy to lose sight of the impact of a child's early, traumatic experiences. Especially if behaviour resembles common parenting challenges, such as rudeness, lack of co-operation or obsession with electronics, it might be hard to "err on the side of trauma". Of course, a child who is adopted or who lives with foster or kinship carers can also be testing the boundaries, be selfish or bad mannered, just like any other

SECTION I

child. However, if usual parenting strategies just do not seem to work, it is wise to presume that the behaviour is related to early traumatic experiences.

If Rebecca and Magda can be supported to see Jayden as a frightened child, rather than as aggressive or violent, it may be easier for them to use a more therapeutic parenting style. That is not to say that they are not therapeutic or nurturing in their approach now, but the stress of living with CPVA can make it hard for parents to think about what may be communicated through behaviour.

For example, Jayden will need his mums to take the initiative to "repair" the relationship after CPVA incidents. Repair refers to any action that lets Jayden know that he is still loved and cared for and that the incident has not damaged or ended their relationship. That may be difficult for Rebecca and Magda, as it may feel like a lack of consequence or even a reward for CPVA. They may need support to see Jayden's behaviour as an expression of distress. They may not be able to forgive and forget immediately, but a smile, a hand on the shoulder or offering him a drink can all communicate that they still care about him.

Jayden is also likely to need extra support and nurture to recover after incidents. He will probably feel exhausted after a prolonged period of dysregulation and may be deeply ashamed of his actions. Appropriate repair and recovery activities in the immediate aftermath of CPVA include staying close to Jayden, while giving him space to rest and reflect. His mums might, for example, watch a TV programme with him with a snack. Some children are so tired after incidents that they fall asleep. Rebecca and Magda may need to be reminded that it can take several hours for Jayden's hormonal balance to return to base level after being in a survival state. This means that it is better to postpone talking about the incident and to resist going over who did or said what, unless

Jayden initiates the conversation. Once he has fully calmed and has had an opportunity to rest, Magda and Rebecca may consider activities that allow Jayden to repair some of the physical and emotional damage he caused. This could include helping to tidy up items that got thrown or broken, or apologising.

Suggested school support

Even though, on the face of it, Jayden seems to be coping well at school, it may benefit the whole family if support can be offered to his teachers. Many children who have experienced early trauma present as compliant and quiet at school but release the difficult emotions that have been building up during the school day once they get back home. They simply do not feel safe enough to show their true emotions at school. It could help Jayden if the adults in his school understood that his compliance might be fuelled by fear, not contentment. Perhaps being at school is an unconscious reminder of all the different adults who once cared for him, but who disappeared from his life: the friends, family and neighbours who looked after him as a baby, his foster carers and his social workers. Only when he is reunited with his mums, the people he feels safest with, can he finally release the stress and exhaustion of trying to be "good" all day. If Jayden can be supported to feel safer in school, he may feel able to express himself more clearly during the school day, and reduce the pressure he probably feels. Hopefully this would also lessen the angry outbursts after school.

Support for school staff might consist of a staff training session on issues affecting children who are adopted, in kinship or foster care, such as attachment difficulties and the impact of early trauma on child development. Additionally, a meeting might be facilitated by an appropriately trained professional with relevant school staff and Jayden's parents. The first aim would be to share information to help school staff to recognise how Jayden is feeling: calm, anxious, unsettled, or angry. His parents will play a key role, because they witness the violent and aggressive behaviour, and because they are the experts regarding their son's feelings.

The second aim would be to plan how Jayden can be supported: how to help him to stay calm when he is calm; how to help him when he is feeling anxious, and how to protect him and everybody else when he is overwhelmed with anger. This plan might need to be reviewed every three to six months, as Jayden's needs will change and as he develops and moves through the school years.

A well informed, empathic and nurturing school environment can make a considerable difference to a child's well-being, as well as to the functioning of a family. The relationship between home and school will become more effective if teachers are aware of the challenges that Jayden and his mums experience at home.

Suggested therapeutic support

Jayden appeared to benefit from Theraplay, but became dysregulated after the sessions. One possible explanation for this could be that some of the activities or games may have been too stimulating for Jayden's sensory processing system. Based on what we know about Jayden's early experiences, we might guess that the development of his sensory system would have been affected by a lack of stimulation and chronic stress. A sensory processing assessment or sensory processing-focused intervention may give Rebecca and Magda more information about the impact of sounds, smells, touch, visual stimuli or movements on Jayden's body and mind. This may help them to make Jayden's environment a little more comfortable for him and to add or remove activities to help soothe his nervous system. For example, he might be calmed by big, strong bear hugs (rather than light touch), or by regularly dangling off a pull-up bar. These insights could also lead to Theraplay sessions being adapted to meet Jayden's sensory needs. Theraplay is just one of a wide range of therapeutic interventions for children and their parents or carers, and families may benefit from the advice of a social worker or clinical psychologist on the best option for their child.

Jayden may furthermore benefit from some of the strategies described in this book, such as developing an awareness of his anger and an understanding that even though he at times hurts and frightens his parents, he is not a bad person. With help from his mums (or a suitable trained and experienced professional), Jayden may be able to make sense of how what happened to him as a very young boy sometimes still makes him feel unsafe, and how CPVA might then feel like the only way he has to defend himself. If Jayden can be supported to feel less ashamed about CPVA, he may become brave enough to experiment with other ways of dealing with difficult or scary situations. For example, when he is in a calm state, his parents might encourage him to help them think of better ways to manage coming off his electronic devices. For example, they could say: 'Jayden, we've noticed that you find it really annoying when we tell you it's time to put your tablet away. I wonder, does it feel like we're telling you off? Let's try and think of another way to end your screen time that is less annoying.'

Suggested support for parents

Lastly, Rebecca and Magda would almost certainly benefit from therapeutic parenting support. Parenting a child who expresses their distress through CPVA can be exhausting, frustrating and upsetting. Understandably, it can have a detrimental effect on the way parents feel about being with their child. In this case, Rebecca seems to be especially affected by the stress of CPVA. She has started to avoid Jayden and has a physical stress response each time Jayden raises his voice, even when he is happy. These are unconscious responses and a sign that she needs support in managing CPVA, rather than a sign that she no longer cares for Jayden. Continued challenge and rejection from a child can affect the level of satisfaction a parent gets from the relationship, which can make parents feel hopeless and make it difficult for parents to feel loving and empathic towards their child (Hughes, 2007). Reminders of extremely difficult times, such as when Jayden almost pushed Rebecca down the stairs, can trigger a survival response in the parent, making it much harder to respond to the child in a therapeutic, or even rational manner.

Professional support would be focused on acknowledging Rebecca's feelings and helping her to understand both Jayden's and her own responses as symptoms of (secondary) trauma (see Glossary). Rebecca needs to be able to share her feelings without fear of judgement, as she is likely to feel ashamed of her changed emotions towards her son. She needs to hear that many other parents living with CPVA feel as she does, but also that there is hope that she will not always feel this way. Professional support might encourage her to start to notice any enjoyable and calm moments with Jayden. Focusing on those times might help rebuild their relationship, and act as a buffer in difficult times.

Magda may also need therapeutic parenting support. She picks Jayden up from school and takes him to therapy sessions. It is likely that she has been taking on more parenting tasks since Rebecca has started distancing herself from Jayden. This might mean that she is frequently exposed to Jayden's distress and anger, which may raise her stress levels. And when one parent becomes less therapeutic in their parenting, the other tends to compensate with extra nurture and understanding. Magda might therefore find herself defending Jayden's behaviour to Rebecca, which may then limit her opportunities to express her own sadness and frustration and leave her in quite an isolated position.

It is clear to see that CPVA can have a negative impact on the couple relationship. For example, this case study suggests that Magda and Rebecca have different opinions about the use of consequences for CPVA incidents. Such differences can easily become a source of conflict, especially if both parents are tired, stressed, and worried about the family's future. Jayden's foster carers separated after he moved out. Although we don't know their reason for this breakup, Rebecca and Magda may wonder, in their darkest moments, whether it might have been caused by the strain of parenting Jayden. They might worry that something similar will eventually happen to them.

Having lived with foster carers who were experiencing relationship difficulties, Jayden may now be hypervigilant regarding any conflict between Magda and Rebecca. This means that therapeutic parenting support for Rebecca and Magda would not only benefit the adults' well-being, but would hopefully also create a calmer, more stable family environment for Jayden.

Police involvement

For very serious and prolonged CPVA incidents, parents may need to consider contacting the police to keep everyone safe. Parents, carers and professionals are often reluctant to involve the police in CPVA incidents. However, many families benefit from their support. Nobody wants to criminalise a traumatised child's survival behaviours, but the arrival of police officers could both de-escalate situations and ensure the safety of all members of the family. Jayden's parents may choose to pro-actively contact community police officers to inform them of the challenges they face as a family, as well as the reasons why Jayden may respond with CPVA. This would allow the police to develop an understanding of the family's needs, as well as providing advice on who to contact in a crisis.

Children will need lots of support after a police visit, especially if they have had scary experiences involving police in their early lives. They may have seen their parents getting arrested or, like Jayden, may have been removed from their first home by police officers. They need to know that police officers came this time to keep everyone safe, not to take them away.

Conclusion

The case study in the previous chapter illustrates that support for families living with CPVA often needs to be multi-faceted. Professionals working with such families must be experienced in supporting children who live in adoptive, foster or kinship families, as well as trained and experienced in working with children who have experienced developmental trauma. Professional support is available from adoption support services, fostering and kinship support services, local authority children's services, and children's charities. The job title of the person offering support is far less important than their experience and attitude towards working with CPVA. The principles discussed in Chapter 3 form a useful guide for anyone parenting, caring for, or working with a child who expresses their distress through CPVA. They cannot be repeated too often:

- The child is not able to stop using violence and aggression by choice.

- CPVA is too complex to be addressed by simple or "quick fix" strategies.

- As this is a developmental issue, parenting approaches and strategies will need to be continually adapted to the child's age and stage of development.

The child-centred strategies in this book may feel to some parents and carers as if they are too "soft" to deal with a difficult and distressing situation such as CPVA. It is understandable that parents and carers who live with CPVA might wish for strategies that target the problem directly, such as "anger management" or removing items or privileges each time a child fails to manage their upset without violence or aggression. However, we understand that while such strategies might briefly seem to work, they are likely to raise children's anxiety levels, as they start to fear what might happen the next time they are unable to control their responses. If CPVA is rooted in an unconscious lack of safety, then no strategy that makes the child's relationship with parents or carers feel less safe will address the root of the problem. In fact, strategies that rely on shame, ignoring feelings or making children feel that they are "bad" are likely to make things worse in the long term.

As discussed throughout this book, when children have experienced developmental trauma, violent and aggressive behaviour is often an expression of the fear, sadness and shame they feel. This means that we need to focus on the underlying causes of distress, rather than just the behaviour we can see. This is why the focus in this book is on strategies that help children to feel safer and to increase their awareness of emotions and physical sensations; strategies that develop the understanding that they are special, precious and loveable, and that there is so much more to them than CPVA. And most importantly, that there is hope that they will in time be able to manage difficult emotions without CPVA.

PARENTING CHILDREN AFFECTED BY CPVA

It's raining shoes and mangoes

Emma and Will Turner

Have you ever had a pile of shoes thrown at you with such force that you've had to move like James Bond to avoid being hit? Have you ever wondered if you were trying to stop a small child from biting you or perhaps fending off a rabid dog? Have you ever wished you'd never made that first call to the adoption agency and then been immediately overwhelmed with feelings of guilt and shame? Have you ever been so frustrated that you've drop-kicked a mango down the hallway? We have.

Who are we?

We were a family of four: mum Emma, dad Will, each with a birth daughter from a previous marriage.

We had been together for four years when we decided to adopt. Our daughters were aged eleven and eight.

We had not intended to have more children; however, as the years passed and life became settled, we felt that we had missed out on raising a child together. Being a step-parent/blended family brings very different challenges and joys. I had raised my daughter alone after my first husband left whilst I was pregnant, and Will had years of contact/custody battles with his ex-wife, so we were both battle-scarred and felt apprehensive as well as excited about the prospect of having another child.

It was one sunny Sunday afternoon when Will brought up the idea of adoption. Both girls were with their other parents and we were sitting in the garden with a beer, feeling grateful for what we had, but realising that we had so much more we could offer. The seed was planted and we started to research. Wow, what an emotional experience that was, all those faces, names, stories!

We are great talkers about ideas, dreams and plans; some we make happen, some we talk about until we decide, 'No, that's not for us'. But this conversation about adoption, like our talks about moving in together, getting married, and years later quitting jobs to go travelling for a year, this "feeling" had grabbed us and we knew that there was a little boy out there who needed us as much as we wanted him!

We always knew it was going to be a boy. Our daughters needed to know that they were our most important and favourite girls, and our boy would need to know that he was our most important and favourite boy. We also knew that we didn't need to have a baby.

We had a fantastic adoption service from our chosen local authority, and looking back, knowing what we know now, I think they knew that our boy was the boy for us. We were experienced parents who both, at the time, worked for the police, so knew a little already about the type of background that adopted children might come from.

Our son, James, was only around two months old when he was taken from his birth family. By the time we made that call to the local authority, he would have been two years and ten months old and he was already classed as a "difficult to place" child because of his severe attachment issues after two failed adoption plans, one after moving in and one during introductions. He had been separated from his half-siblings when he was a year old, and he had 12 moves in care; he was quite famous in the local authority, but here we were: a family that the adoption team thought might just be the one for him.

Our son-to-be had just moved into a new foster home at this point, with an experienced foster carer who had other older children on long-term special guardianship orders, so perhaps James was also on course for a life in care.

But then, instead, our son was assigned a therapeutic social worker to prepare him for having a family, and we have continued to work with this person over the years, aided by the Adoption Support Fund.

Identifying our son

Part of our pre-adoption course was on what to expect when you get to the matching process. Profiles of three or four different children were given to us in a bundle, so that we could see the kind of information that was shared with prospective adopters. Each child had a little booklet, with pictures and sections about likes/dislikes, character, brief background and what type of family would suit them. Think dating page mixed with a house brochure and you get the idea! Two of the profiles were of little boys: one around the age we thought would fit in with our family, and another slightly younger; that slightly younger one had a cheeky glint in his eyes and a smile that seemed to have an infectious laugh behind it. Those are now the eyes that seek us out in times of joy and sadness, and that smile really does have an infectious and naughty laugh behind it. Despite what our social workers say, we don't think it was a coincidence that his profile was in our bundle, or that his family-finder ended up becoming our adoption social worker.

We talked about the profiles on the way home from the course, and James' image wouldn't leave us; it was just like how you imagine your child before they are born. So James started to be imagined into our lives. The next day on our course, we spoke to his family-finder and our social worker, Julia. We said that we were willing to change our age range for the right boy and that James could be the right boy. Because we were still on the course, nothing could move, but we were given a little bit more information about James' background. We had already been seduced by the photos of his dirty, chubby face, his "naughtiness" captured on camera, those eyes and that cheeky grin.

After the course finished and we started the adoption process with Julia, we approached this part of adoption like we do most things in life: if something needs doing just get on and do it, no point moaning and complaining and it's not the time to try and fight the system. If you are going to spend time arguing about why you need to get rid of your pond, then I would suggest that you need to save that energy for things that really matter. When we are bringing some of our society's most vulnerable children into our homes, we need to accept that there are good reasons behind the policies and procedures that are in place to protect us all.

We are straight talkers, so we were fortunate to get on really well with the social workers, who told us things as they needed to be told. James wasn't ready for a new mummy and daddy just yet; they told us to trust the process and see where everyone was when decisions had to be made. Once it was clear that we should and would go ahead, James' social worker came to tell us more about him. Whether adoption or long-term foster care was the decision, it would have to be James' last move. We were given a "warts and all" account of his birth family history and his time in care. It was made very clear to us that this was not going to be an easy journey. However, there would be lots of support to make this next move a successful one. What was not mentioned was the possibility of child to parent violence. It was not recorded as part of James' history nor of his siblings' history. We did learn of sibling violence, and this was described as "rough play" and "controlling behaviour" and a reason why the siblings could not be placed together. It wasn't until much later that we realised it wasn't just rough play, but intentional hurt inflicted on James by his older brother.

We carried on with the process and we were asked if we would like to trial an unusual way of meeting James; the plan was to "accidentally on purpose" be in the same place at the same time.

73

We met with James' foster carer prior to seeing him, so we knew who to look out for. When we saw him, he was on a contact day out with his brother, it was just before Christmas and our first vision of this chubby three-year-old was his little bobble hat running up and down the queue to see Santa and trying to post his older brother's head into a giant letter-box. We were smitten! He came over as we were talking to his foster carer and immediately asked, 'Who are they?' The carer explained that we were friends, but I don't believe that James believed that for one minute; he's very intuitive, but he played along, and like most young children was drawn to Will and his beard. He asked, 'Are you a baby?' causing much laughter about the idea of huge baby Will with a big ginger beard. We left them to enjoy the rest of their Santa visit and headed to the café. They followed a short while later. 'What are you doing here, again?', James shouted in his biggest little deep voice. We watched him demolish his lunch, apple core and all, and be very boisterous around the café. Then he and his brother came over to chat to us. We left them after that and headed to the car to call Julia and tell her, 'He is the boy for us'. James loves this story and it is one we often recount in times of uncertainty when he needs reassurance.

It was a couple of months after this that we headed to the adoption panel to be approved as adopters. However, the local authority ran the matching process alongside, so that two weeks after approval we went to the matching panel, and we got a unanimous vote to become James' parents.

74

Introductions

Introductions were planned to be over a four-week period. This was a new and longer procedure than usual, and we were going to be the trial family because of James' two previous failed adoptions.

Introductions started with a cup of tea in the foster carer's home. A few days later we went for coffee and baked a cake together; the next visit was a trip to the park with the foster carer, and eventually we led up to taking James out on our own. We took him to a park and a play barn, and it was so hard not to scoop him up to hug him, but we had to take it slowly and build trust.

James' first visit to our home was with his foster carer, and on a following visit our girls were present for five minutes before their grandparents took them out. During the third week James was starting to ask questions, such as, 'Why are you here so much?', 'Why are you taking me out?', 'Are you my new mummy and daddy?' Led by the professionals, we answered with, 'Would you like us to be?', 'Maybe we should ask if we can be?' James was starting to become distressed, so the timeline shifted and he was told that yes, we would like to be his parents, and we started to bring and leave some of his things in our house after visits. We shopped for things for his bedroom and we had a mini day out together with our daughters. He started to get upset when we left him, but he was also upset about leaving his foster family. On his last evening with them, we joined in a little celebration, and the next day they dropped him off at his new home with the rest of his belongings. It was heartbreaking and exciting at the same time. I don't think we slept that first night because we kept checking on him. But he slept soundly for a few nights before the night terrors we had been warned about came back, and so did our sleepless nights while we sat with him and listened to his nightmares and helped him to get back to sleep.

In the beginning

We were warned that this little boy, who by the time he came to live with us was aged three-and-a-half, would probably never call us Mummy and Daddy, and that attachments would be hard to build. He was Mr Independent, and in his head he could have set himself up in a flat and managed his life by himself; he was not wanting to be parented!

We had to teach him what "good" mummies and daddies do, little things like helping him put his shoes on or wiping his bottom. I remember his foster carer saying, 'He can do his own shoes', but he needed to learn that yes, he could, but he didn't have to, not any more. There were, and still are, so many opportunities to teach him what good mums and dads do.

James wasn't a particularly small child and I'm not a particularly big person, but wrapping this chubby little boy in a towel after his bath, and carrying him like you would a baby, was exactly what we both needed. When Dad hurt his back carrying him and I could only piggy-back him for a short time, we bought a pushchair for him, which helped with the bonding; however, it didn't help the framework of the pushchair, as he exceeded its weight limit.

Some of our fondest memories, and one that we were

recently reminded of, are about James' bedtime routine when he first moved in. He used to have a bottle of milk while watching *In the Night Garden* and we started off by sitting either side of him, not touching, but every night we edged a little closer until, like in some romantic movie, our fingers touched, and then before he realised, we held hands, and this went on for a while until he was ready to sit snuggled up as close as possible. "Huggles" became one of his favourite things.

The reason we were reminded about this is because one of his recent "meltdowns" resulted in him withdrawing from us; he wouldn't let us comfort him physically, and he self-punished by refusing all care. He was exhausted, so we managed to get him to go to bed and started off sitting by the door, refusing to leave him because we are "good parents" and 'You don't have to do this alone, but we respect that you don't want us near you'. Then I edged towards the bed, then I put one arm on the bed, then I laid my hand on his shoulder. I moved back if he resisted, but tried again before long. I reminded him of the story of his early bedtime routine and how we would just go at his pace. Eventually we ended up having a huge family hug on his bed.

The problem about calling us Mummy and Daddy was resolved by our daughters. They wanted to know how to refer to us when talking to their new little brother. They don't call us by our first names, so we told them to say what came naturally, which was Mummy/Daddy, and that's what stuck. At first it was just a name to call us by, but as time went on, he claimed us as his mummy and daddy: cows in fields would be introduced to: 'Mummy and Daddy and me'. And then he began to include his sisters; he was claiming his family and began

77

role-playing family scenarios with his toys. These role plays nearly always took on some form of protective element.

How child to parent violence started

It started very gradually, and it started very much like a toddler's tantrum. James would try to hit us, pull our hair and scratch. At the time, we thought that it was part of his attachment difficulty and responded as you would to a toddler, with verbal cues reminding him that this is not acceptable. However, as it got worse and he was, and still is, incredibly strong, we realised that this wasn't something we had seen before, and something more was going on.

The first time I was injured was when I was trying to keep him safe by holding his hand while crossing a busy car park, while he wanted to run off. As I held on to his hand, his nails dug into my skin and I still have that scar today, along with a few others from when I've not kept those nails short enough. Hair pulling has resulted in chunks of hair being pulled from his sisters' heads. However, with Dad, who is over six feet tall, and as James puts it, is 'my big strong Daddy', he fights by punching and rhino-charging him.

When James was feeling insecure and became aggressive, he was not safe to be left alone, because he would smash anything breakable. He has always had a good throwing arm and anything that he could pick up could be launched through the air. He also knows what triggers people, so he would draw on a sister's homework, throw something at a sister or harass the dog to provoke a reaction. Being left doesn't help him calm down; he just ups the ante. James is very skilled at knowing how to charm people, and as a small child charmed many a waitress into giving him a free ice cream. The flip side of this is that he is equally skilled at knowing that targeting Mum will get a reaction from Dad, and targeting sisters will get a reaction from Mum, and so on. In these situations, we would try to focus on his intended target rather than his behaviour, but whoever stayed with him would be subject to the entire contents of a room thrown at them – at least, whatever came to hand and whatever he could pick up, like sofa cushions, shoes, books, anything that was nearby and would cause the most harm or upset. He once threw a hairbrush across the room at me, and it hit a large picture on the wall and shattered the glass; that shocked and scared him and the emotional repair was much quicker that day.

We have been to lots of courses on child to parent violence and tried out lots of different techniques; some worked and some didn't; some worked for a period of time, but then James would get wise to it, so we had to change track, as he did.

I remember being told that, 'Being the only person to lose control can feel like being in a very lonely place', so when we are feeling calm enough we will raise our energy to match his. One very memorable occasion was when he was throwing a stuffed hedgehog doorstop around our bedroom, aiming at me. He was angry, he was angry that he got hurt when he was a baby, he was angry that his birth parents couldn't keep him safe, that his birth family didn't go to jail, that he was in foster care, and I could see how it was leading to uncontrollable anger that would result in broken items

79

or James trying to scratch, punch or throw things at me. No matter what I tried to calm him, it wasn't working, so I also started throwing this poor hedgehog around, and shouting at it that I was angry too. We took it in turns to say what we were angry about: I was angry that he was angry, I was angry that I wasn't there to protect him when he was a baby, angry that it took us so long to find each other. After a while I helped him to turn it around and to focus on what we did have: we were now together as a family and we knew how to look after children and keep them safe. He said that he had had enough, we said our thanks to the hedgehog, and then we started "the repair".

To repair is often to engage or encourage regression: younger-type play or games and offering nurture as you would to a younger child; lots of cuddles and talking about nice times in the past, reminding James how far we have all come, that we are a family and family means that we love each other even if sometimes we don't like each other. We tell him that he is still a child, and a child who has had to deal with many difficulties, so we expect him to get things wrong. However, if he hurts us, there are consequences. We try not to do reward and punishment, but consequences are a part of life, and he needs boundaries. Being able to maintain boundaries is one reason we were chosen for him.

Valuing physical strength and weapons

Early into the adoption, we noticed that our son placed a very high value on physical strength. In his mind, the person who was biggest and strongest was the person who should be in charge. When he was playing with other children, he would ingratiate himself with the biggest and oldest boy. He also always wanted to have some sort of weapon. At first it seemed cute that he wanted to carry his little umbrella with him everywhere, until we realised that he thought it offered him some kind of protection. He could and still can weaponise anything; he'd even nibble his toast into the shape of a gun or a sword. As young as 11, he'd say, 'Look, I've made a gun', and show you something that he'd cobbled together out of bits of Lego and things he's found in his pockets.

When things are bad and he's got himself wound up, he will appear wearing a robot mask and carrying an array of weapons such as a Nerf gun or a plastic light-saber (if they've not been confiscated or you didn't make it to the toy cupboard before he did!), usually strapped to his body with belts, making him look like an extra from a budget sci-fi movie. He will then stand in the doorway trying to strike fear into our hearts. In truth it's very draining, as we know we are in for an hour or so of having sponge darts fired at us while he runs up and down the stairs yelling what terrible parents we are. Several years ago, he would aim the sponge darts directly at us and we ended up having to remove all fighting toys; it's only recently they have made a return. Now he shoots in our general direction, but not at us, or aims at our feet.

He never uses anything now that would cause real injury. In fact, we can now trust him with something genuinely dangerous, such as a sharp knife in the kitchen, an axe, or an air rifle, and when we do, he is incredibly careful.

We were once on holiday and there was the usual

evening family entertainment. Two people were dressed in child-friendly seagull and lizard costumes. We thought James might enjoy it – how wrong we were! When he saw the characters, he clung to Dad and wouldn't join in with the other children. He said, 'I want to stay with my big, strong Daddy. Daddy, you can kill them if you want.' We then had to have a whole conversation about how we could keep him safe without resorting to killing the seagull and the lizard…even if their songs were really annoying.

For James, there is a mismatch between perceived threats and genuine dangers. He is still nervous about going upstairs on his own in the dark, and his imagination runs riot. His biggest fears for a long time were the Cat in the Hat and the Grinch. The thought of these characters still sends a shudder down his spine. However, we took him travelling and he'd happily skip through a sprawling, noisy, seemingly hostile, chaotic Latin American city at night with not a care in the world.

The obsession with strength led his early play. He liked to pretend to be an animal and would usually choose to be a rhino or a silverback gorilla. When he first came to us, and suffered from night terrors, he would wake up having dreamt that he was alone in a jungle and giant spiders were after him.

When he first met our therapeutic social worker, whilst still in foster care, they played a game whereby he hid under the bed covers, and then when he appeared, he would roar at her, letting her know how big, brave and strong he was. Roaring continues to be a way to express himself, and he can do an awesome T-Rex from *Jurassic Park*.

82

We enjoy watching nature documentaries together, like David Attenborough's *Dynasties* series, particularly the one about a chimp family with an alpha male called David. This is often the best way to describe what our home life occasionally looks like, with our son constantly charging around vying for the alpha position. It turns out that this is something that genuinely worries him. Only a few weeks ago, we remarked about how he had grown very broad and strong, when he said, 'Remember the alpha chimp, Dad? He got old and his son fought him and he was badly hurt. I worry that will happen to us.' Logically, he knows that we aren't a band of chimps and don't have to have a fight to the death to be top, but it still worries him.

The "comedown" and "repair"

The "comedown" from these intense periods of physical or verbal aggression has left us feeling physically and mentally exhausted, sad for James and for ourselves. The guilt that we could have handled it better could knock us off kilter for hours. We had to remember that we needed the "comedown" to repair and feel balanced again. It took a long time to accept that and not to beat ourselves up because we had not done what we had set out to do that day (housework, provide a nourishing meal, time to play, and time to spend as a family).

We found that sometimes, after an outburst, our son could calm down and return to a normal balance quicker than we could. He would be fine while we were still feeling distressed and struggling to come to terms with the situation. He would be confused about why everything wasn't back to normal.

83

Strategies

Bad acting

This is a strategy that works for us when we foresee flash points that could build up to aggression and violence. We found that we could manipulate situations by "play arguing" with each other: one parent would list all the reasons why James should not do something (giving the parental point of view), and the other would disagree and give all the reasons why James should be allowed to do it. "It" would be something like James wanting to ride his bike on his own to his tennis lesson. One parent would say why they thought it could go wrong, and the other would say what could be done to mitigate the risks if James were to agree to certain ground rules. The aim was a happy compromise, which meant that James was allowed to do the thing he wanted to do, but without becoming angry and potentially physically or verbally aggressive about the ground rules. We always make it clear that we don't raise our voices or become disrespectful to each other, for we are modelling how to have differing opinions and come to a satisfactory compromise without physical or verbal aggression. It sounds very odd describing it now, and we definitely wouldn't win any awards for our acting ability, but it was one of the strategies that usually seemed to work.

Emotions

Being told "no/wait/stop" makes James feel frustrated. Now that he is older, he can often ask 'why?' and if he understands the reason or that we aren't saying 'no' forever, it will help to defuse a situation. When he was younger, any frustration led to quick outbursts of violence or aggressive behaviour. We helped James to label his feelings and to understand that emotions make us human and that one emotion does not define us, so being angry is just part of him like it is of all of us, and that he is also made up of humour, kindness, love and sadness, etc. He is now very emotionally intelligent and can let us know that he is angry with us for a specific reason or something is making him sad or happy. He is also good at picking up on emotions in other people, and he can be very empathetic, or sometimes, if he's in a devious mood, he will use his insight to aggravate.

Self-care

Although he can't tell you why, it unsettles James when either Mum or Dad are ill. We have reassured him that he does not need to feel unsafe because we will not become too ill to look after him, but it disturbs him enough to become super helpful until we can't do anything for him, and then he becomes aggressive.

Having down days ourselves is often hard, as James will sense that too, and if it makes him feel insecure, it can lead to aggression when we are least able to cope. So we have to make sure we look after ourselves to minimise these down periods, and we are learning to ask for help from friends and family. I suggest you do this sooner rather than later so that you don't get too run down like we did! Self-care is a strategy for helping our children.

Having a plan

Our therapeutic social worker helped us to write a family safety plan, which included the girls going to their rooms, and a family member being called if Dad wasn't around and things were escalating.

SECTION II

When James was eight, we even introduced ourselves to the local police officer and explained our situation, because as James was getting bigger, stronger and louder, there was every chance that a neighbour would call the police to report domestic abuse. As we both worked for the police, this was probably less strange for James and us than it might have been otherwise. It helps James to understand that there are other people out there to keep him and us safe, and we have never needed to call for help from the police. Our neighbours are aware of at least part of our situation, and are supportive.

We have worked on this plan with James, so that he knows if his behaviour becomes dangerous, we will need to put the dog in her cage, sisters (when they are at home) will go to their room and we may call a grandparent to come and assist. He doesn't usually become fully aggressive or violent in front of others, and when Grandpa has had to come, James has hidden under a chair and refused to come out until Grandpa has gone. It is not a strategy that we like to use as it can be shameful to admit that your child is violent towards you, and you don't want others to judge them. Some of our immediate family don't even know the extent of our situation, because judgements can be made that are not based on an understanding of James' early life trauma and his inability to express himself safely.

Not reacting to provocation
Much, much easier said than done! This one is for when you feel that whatever is being directed at you is fairly low level and you, your loved ones, pets and your favourite ornaments are not likely to come to any harm. An example of James trying to provoke is when he has

got to the stage of name-calling, questioning your parenting abilities, swearing, throwing soft objects or a bit of light spitting. If you can see it for what it actually is, and not get caught up in the emotional side of it, then you can ride it out. Ask yourself if being pelted with socks or (clean) underpants is really that bad – are you going to come to any harm? Probably not. Is a spot of light spitting from a small child particularly disgusting? They've not got the range, volume or level of accuracy to make it truly vile. You've dealt with worse when you've had to clean up their sick, snot, poo, etc. It could be appropriate to don an expression of unflappability and sit there with a pair of undies on your head while calmly drinking a cup of tea. You never know, the ridiculousness of the situation might make even an angry child laugh.

Using humour

One to get in quick when you feel that things are building up. This is a hard one to describe as every situation is different and everyone's sense of humour is different. It could be something as simple as James launching himself on me in an attempt to hurt me, but being quickly able to turn it into play by my blowing a raspberry on his belly. At other times we can share the funny side of the situation, like the time he covered himself in blue electrical tape thinking that it would make him look terrifying (it didn't!). Shared laughter can be healing.

Holding

Something else we found that helped during times of high anxiety and feeling unsafe was if his dad wrapped and held him in a bear hug so he couldn't escape. It sounds like physical restraint but it is more of an extreme cuddle, and James still finds it comforting, although he uses all his strength to try to break free. It is a strategy to demonstrate that Dad is strong enough to keep James safe.

Thankfully, he needs fewer and fewer bear-hugs, because as he's becoming such a big strong boy, it becomes more and more difficult to hold him. Will that raise questions about us being able to keep James safe, or will it signal that he is strong enough to protect himself?

Even after eight years as a family, we sometimes have to revert back to those early ways to reassure James in order to prevent child to parent violence. When he won't allow us to come close, we talk about when he first arrived, sitting on the couch together, and edging closer to him, until he would finally let us in for a big cuddle.

"Hurty Hands"

Hurty Hands is a term we used for when James would hurt us or break things, or his fists would clench in readiness. We taught him to blow on his hands to blow the anger away. This helped him to visualise his anger leaving and also helped to regulate his breathing.

Sports and physical activity

We found that high energy physical activity, especially contact sports run by someone who makes it well-disciplined fun, really helped. We deliberately steered James away from martial arts that involved punching and kicking, for fear that in a moment of anger he would use these skills against us. Sports that involved some sort of grappling worked well for James. Judo was very good and the instructor kept a nice balance between strong discipline and fun. It appealed to James's view of physical size and strength that the coach was built like a brick outhouse, but could be gentle and let the young children practice their judo throws on him.

We tried rugby when the age restrictions only allowed James to take part in tag rugby, which didn't really interest him that much. It was apparent from an early age that our boy was built for power, not speed. We went back to rugby when he was old enough for the full contact game. The coaches are all dads who give up their time at the weekend. Again, they make it fun, but in a disciplined environment, fostering respect for other players, the referee and for the rules of the game. James really got into the physicality of the game and rapidly became a good player. The coaches praised his physical strength, but as parents who had experienced first-hand his full strength, we could tell that he was holding back. We could see that during some tackles he was letting himself fall to the ground without much resistance. It turned out that we had done such a good job in helping him with his "Hurty Hands" that he didn't know when and how he could use aggression in a controlled environment.

We talked to James about using his full strength, and he said that he was worried about hurting the other players. We discussed when it was appropriate to use physical strength in a controlled environment within the confines and rules of the game. It was as if he needed our permission: if Mum and Dad say I can charge like a rhino, then it must be OK. What is interesting is that we can see him moderate the power of his tackles according to the size of the opposition player, going in a little softer against the smaller boys. That first full season of rugby, he won the coach's award for most improved player. He was so shocked and proud that he won; it was a good job we were wearing sunglasses to hide the tears streaming down our faces.

A surprise sport that was born out of swing ball in the garden during the Covid-19 lockdowns was James' desire to play tennis. Although tennis is about as far as you can get from a contact sport, we believe it has also helped him to use controlled aggression under the right circumstances and within the strict confines of the game. Once more, the coach is a young guy who is fun but disciplined.

Encouraging our son to participate in the right kind of physical activity has helped him to make use of his abundance of energy and to learn that aggression can be controlled and used in an appropriate setting and at the appropriate time. We're not saying that sport is an instant fix for child to parent violence, but we believe that it is one of many strategies that have gone some way to helping our family. Sport has also given James a sense of pride in what he has achieved by his own merit. He has learned to be a good loser and a gracious winner, except when he plays with us; then he manages to be both a terrible loser and an unbearable winner! We hope that is because he feels totally safe within the confines of our family unit.

Dealing with verbal aggression
As the physical violence decreased over time, we noticed that the verbal aggression was getting worse. James does now choose to use words to hurt rather than physical violence. He will regularly unleash a barrage of insults, foul language and threats. This is a

huge step forward and means we are physically safer as a family, but that is not to say that words can't hurt too, and be as emotionally draining.

Humour works well to defuse a situation, but you have to be in the right place yourself to use this tactic. We found that ignoring behaviour does not work at all, and James will escalate the verbal assault in content, foul language and volume. We try to acknowledge his feelings but clearly state that our rules, about what is acceptable, still apply. This is work in progress and we are seeking further help as James heads towards being a teenager.

Wishing you'd never adopted and soul-crushing guilt
Wishing that you'd never adopted your child feels like a taboo subject in the world of adoption. Readers may be able to tell me it is common. But for those people riding the ups and downs of adoption, it can feel like you are the only person who feels like this. You are not at any point supposed to have those awful thoughts and if you do, you definitely shouldn't go on having them. Just to emphasise how bad you must be for having these thoughts, they are followed by soul-crushing guilt and images of where your child would be now if you hadn't adopted them.

I believe that there is a world of difference between a genuine adoption breakdown and fleeting thoughts that if you hadn't adopted, then you could be sitting in an Italian restaurant drinking coffee rather than trying to explain to strangers in a shop the reason why your child is spitting at you.

The future

Our son has pulled hair from our daughters' heads, kicked and punched Dad, scratched and scarred Mum, thrown a hairbrush at a picture and smashed the glass. We have had "shoe-gate" when every available shoe in the house has been thrown at us, a bedroom barricade, and our son going tooled up with a poker to try and gain entry to a room where his sister was shielding. But we also have a son that loves fiercely, is gentle and truly one of the kindest children I have ever met. He is compassionate and empathetic; but still, if anyone dares to say anything mean about his family, his jaw will clench, his fists will go into tight balls, his shoulders will hunch, and if he doesn't feel safe and secure his survival mode to fight will kick in.

We write this eight years after James joined our family and he is now nearly 12 years old. Today, his fight mode looks very different, much gentler, calmer, more verbal, and we struggle to recall the last time he was violent towards us. Today he may throw a pen in our general direction or a forceful sock, but now he tends to use his voice and words to hurt us, or he will stomp upstairs, slam doors, and quite often use swear words, usually in context, so high five for use of the English language!

We are in a fortunate place because we can be proactive as we approach the teen years. We are starting to look at "parenting adolescents" courses and have booked sessions with our therapeutic social worker for James and us to help us navigate the next stages: progression through secondary school, contact with James' birth sibling, puberty, and a deeper understanding of his own life story.

We still have scars as a reminder of violent times, but they also remind us of how far he and we have come and how much we can still achieve. His and our lives have been changed forever, and together as a family we have evolved and will continue to evolve, always with love and always together.

PS: Wish us luck for the teen years, and we wish you and your family a happy and CPV-free life.

It wasn't always like this

Daniel Swanson

George, now ten-and-a-half years old, is sitting on the other side of my studio, with a gigantic mural as his backdrop, surrounded by my ordered artistic chaos. We're singing along to a playlist he made en route to Dorset in the summertime, recalling a family trip in the sunshine, car windows down and singing at the tops of our lungs. George has been focused on a drawing he's making for the past hour, an intended gift for his neighbour friend, and shows no signs of losing concentration. Occasionally he shows me his drawing, asking for advice or simply looking for approval and praise. By complete coincidence, a familiar song is playing (a current favourite of ours), saying that things aren't the same as they were...wow, isn't that the truth.

In the beginning

My husband William and I brought George home from his foster carers right after his fourth birthday party; not the most usual or desirable timing, but it worked for George, and was a sweet affair with his foster family. The afternoon was filled with treats and food otherwise forbidden to him, and with grown-ups who understood better than he did what was about to happen.

Food was a problem, his social worker had said. We knew from all of the reports that George had a background of neglect. Police had once entered the flat and found George, in a nappy, on his own, digging through the rubbish looking for food. Once he was found on his own scrounging for food in leftover pizza boxes from a gathering his birth mother had the night before. We knew about the food thing. George couldn't get enough. He couldn't stop talking about it, and would say he was hungry even as he was stuffing his face. We also knew that George would attach to any stranger he met; he was indiscriminate with his affections, presumably a skill he learned when surrounded by unheeding adults and looking for someone, anyone, to take care of him.

We had also read about the instances of domestic abuse. George must have seen many more things than were in the masses of reports we'd read. Social workers were afraid to do their statutory checks on the family due to gang involvement, so they sent the police instead. We knew George's birth father had head-butted George's mother whilst she was pregnant with George. We also knew that there were instances of choking, biting, kicking and hitting. When asked at the time what he remembered of his birth father, George said, 'I know he had a red beard', and he made a sort of sign language gesture that could be interpreted as red pouring out of a mouth...and considering his birth father didn't have a beard as far as we knew, well, we had our suspicions. The straw that finally broke the camel's back was when George's birth mother was discovered on a London bus, inebriated and covered in blood, clutching two-and-a half-year-old George close to her chest; she was on the run from the perpetrator.

But at his farewell birthday party, surrounded by *Frozen*-themed bunting and birthday cake, hot dogs and other treats, this smiling and incredibly brave four-year-old showed us nothing but confidence and joy.

Luckily, and I think this is the most important takeaway of our story (spoiler alert!), we had help. For the past year or more, William and I had been working with our adoption agency, delving deep into our own past and likely parenting styles, and learning everything we could about the challenges we might face once a child was placed with us. From our agency, we learned about a myriad of possibilities: we were prepared for food issues and the results of neglect, domestic abuse and sexual abuse.

'Boy, George can really throw a tantrum when he wants something', his foster family had said.

'No problem', we'd said, with more confidence than we deserved to have.

'No – really, I've never seen anything like it', they replied.

That was our first hint of what was to come.

Though not actually healthy, it was very handy for our bonding that George was "attachment seeking". His local authority had warned us that he was constantly looking for someone to take care of him (read: keep him safe). Like most prospective adopters, we had made a film for George, to introduce him to his new life, as well as a book of words and photos to help him become familiar with us, our home, our dog and his potential future family and friends. On day one of introductions, George met us at the door with huge hugs, calling us by our chosen names (Daddy and Pops). He certainly broke the ice for us! Later that day or the next, we went for a walk with the foster family and George, who was more than happy to ride on my shoulders and chatter away. At one point, he said to me, 'Daddy, I love you'. Well, as a sensible grown-up, I knew that was impossible so soon, but it certainly endeared us to this charming boy!

Things improved and improved, and after the ten-day introduction period, we were hooked! Apart from George's issue with food, it looked as though this adoption was going to be a walk in the park.

In truth, the first month or so was exhausting. William and I had loved being "fun uncles" in the past, and mistakenly thought that that was what it took to be a good parent. We were "jazz hands a go-go". In one of our many sessions with our adoption agency (now offering post-adoption support), we confessed, almost ashamed, that we were absolutely drained of energy. 'What have you been doing together?' asked our social worker/therapist. We listed a million high-energy (mostly home-based) things we'd done during

SECTION 11

97

this period of getting to know one another. Her eyes widened in surprise. 'I wonder if you might try some calm time...maybe watch a film together?'

As it turned out, at the same time, George nearly fell asleep in his own session, confessing he was 'very tired'.

They had a point.

And then...

As George became more comfortable with us, and his attachment grew, we began to see his other side. Sure enough, George could throw a tantrum beyond that of most birth children. Almost always, these tantrums were associated with little George asking for something he wanted, and if he didn't get it, that is when it happened. Looking back through the post-adoption therapy team's notes, there were indications that George was, under the surface, not as placid as his attachment-seeking, ever-smiley face seemed to show. There were tiny hints, here and there, that George had seen more domestic abuse than his local authority had been willing to say. When dysregulated (see Glossary), George would breathe heavily, widen his eyes, bare his teeth, grimace or completely disassociate and then explode. Slowly but surely, these tantrums became more and more physical. Hitting, biting, kicking, spitting and choking would often accompany a tantrum. As time went on, and George's attachment grew, so did the number and scope of these violent behaviours.

Four months into the placement, at a local Montessori nursery, George hit another child. We hoped that this was an isolated incident. Luckily, the nursery was well aware of George's background and dealt with it very calmly.

Foolishly, we kept the instances of aggression to ourselves for months. They were sporadic, and I suppose we didn't want to acknowledge that there was an underlying issue. Maybe we thought that because we didn't put a name to it, the go-to aggressive behaviour wasn't real, or that by speaking about the aggression out loud we would somehow have failed.

After almost exactly five months of living together, we had a statutory visit from the local authority nurse. By now, we had realised that every time a new outsider appeared for one of these many visits, George would become massively dysregulated. We constantly reminded ourselves that this was understandable. George had experienced such a disruptive infancy, with constant parties full of strangers followed by frequent moves between his birth mother's friends and family, depending on their life situation at the time. George never knew when he'd be moved again at a moment's notice. During this particular visit, George spent the time screaming and jumping on the sofa and throwing things. Earlier in the day he'd bitten me, and hurt William. According to records, this is the first time we admitted to our therapy team that violence was a real concern. Once we could no longer pretend this wasn't an issue, we developed the motto "do the work now for a better future".

Help at hand

Luckily, our post-adoption support had been in place from before day one. Now we were offered frequent

SECTION II

sessions with George together and separately, working on attachment, following suggestions and advice for dealing with violence and aggression. One of the key components of this first stage was Theraplay (see Glossary). The aim of Theraplay was to help increase our family attachments. Anticipating what might be around the corner, sessions always started with sharing our motto and corresponding hand gestures: "no hurts (crossed fingers), stick together (laced fingers), have fun! (jazz hands)".

Whenever there was an incident of physical aggression, we would always have to remain calm, remind George that there were "no hurts", and try to ride it out. We learned that, due to George's background of neglect, he really had no way to soothe himself. If a baby cries in a healthy situation, they will be comforted and calmed, and eventually learn how to soothe themselves. George wouldn't have had that opportunity. His neural pathways simply hadn't developed in that way, which is why his reactions and behaviours had to go over the top before any semblance of self-soothing could take place. At the age of four, we had to treat him as we would a baby.

Pre-adoption, we had taken a two-day course in *The Great Behaviour Breakdown*, which presented an alternative way of interacting with challenging situations. Whereas a traditional approach to "bad" behaviour would call for discipline and punishment, the GBB encouraged us to take the view that those responses only work if the child respects and trusts the carers. The best course of action (at least at first) was to divert attention and change the mood of the situation.

We developed many hilarious ways of dealing with a

tantrum. More than once, if we were in a supermarket or out in the park, and George was in the middle of a meltdown, we would lie down on the ground and throw a 200 per cent comedy tantrum ourselves. Imagine the stares we got from onlookers! There we were, grown adults in public, and rather than discipline our son in a way most people were used to, we would be lying on the ground, making exaggerated whining sounds, writhing about and banging our hands on the ground. The best thing was, that most of the time, it worked! George would snap out of his tantrum and begin to laugh and we could carry on.

Another very helpful alternative technique related to regulation had to do with volume and intensity. If George was screaming at an eight on the scale of loudness, we'd shout at a 10, but in a positive tone, saying things like, 'Wow, you're REALLY showing me that you want to have this thing...', we'd continue speaking, and slowly de-escalate our volume until it was at a normal level. This was incredibly helpful in bringing the intensity down in those difficult situations.

Similarly, our support workers suggested that when George was in a tantrum to scold him loudly and forcefully, telling him off for about 30 seconds, then move directly into repair mode, using a gentle tone.

We paid attention to situations that were triggers and tried to evolve our strategies as we went along. One key slogan we had, at the beginning, was "avoid, inform or remove". We learned to be very thoughtful about our movements, and to avoid high-stimulation environments if at all possible. It was as though we were gazing into a dysregulation crystal ball, trying to plan for all possible outcomes. Wherever there was stimulation was a prime location for a tantrum, and we would decide whether it was best to avoid it, or to inform people concerned of the situation, or, if something was about to kick off (or just had), to remove ourselves. We will probably never know what really happened in George's birth family, but we surmised that George would probably be given whatever he wanted at the grocery store or when out, to avoid a tantrum. Of course, George didn't tell us that; he showed us!

It became clear to us that processed sugar would lead to dysregulation. According to our therapy team and training, this was not a huge surprise. Refined sugar creates a chemical similar to the one our brain produces when we're afraid, whereas protein is more akin to regulating chemicals.

We made sure always to carry high-protein snacks (mostly cheese) to help balance George's brain chemistry. We would often take him to our local park on his scooter. This was great for exercise and for the dog, but frequently led to George running away. And we'd have to watch like a hawk for the ice cream man. Of course, we weren't inhumane when it came to ice cream, but we were advised by the GBB and our support worker to pre-empt such situations. Either avoid the ice cream van, or say, 'Hey – should we get an ice cream?' Thereby showing that we can all have an occasional treat, and that it was our idea, not his.

I, being a home-body anyway, was a huge proponent of the "avoid" tactic. Any sort of shop or store was the most likely location for a four-year-old's atomic reaction, so we did the best we could to have our groceries delivered, or shop on our own whilst the other parent was at home with George. One of the most vivid incidents happened when, seven months into the adoption, I had to pop around the corner to pick up something specific and vital for dinner. I was in a hurry, and saw it as a quick stop-and-grab, but William was not at home, so I had to take George with me. The second he saw the shop, George ran away in the parking lot and dashed into the store on his own. Running away had been a big issue up to this point, as it was scary for us, and unsafe for him. When I finally caught up with him, George insisted I buy him something. I said, 'Not this time, we're just grabbing yoghurt', and George produced a massive tantrum. As per one of our tactics, I put George on my lap in an attempt to soothe him and explain the situation. Unfortunately, George would have none of it, and took this opportunity to slam his head into my chin so hard that I saw stars. Believe me when I say, it was extremely difficult to remain calm while cartoon birdies circled my head. As I recall, I didn't have the presence of mind to put any of our other strategies into place and we left immediately. Dinner was slightly less tasty as a result!

Of course, this was an incident we discussed with our support team, and as always they had great advice. It was to temporarily raise our tone of voice for 30 seconds, not shouting, not being angry, but firm, explaining that something hurt, or why something was unsafe, in an attempt to break the upward emotional escalation. Then we would have to speak soothingly to repair the situation. If we had a snack, that's when we should give it (if we hadn't already...which was often the case, and sometimes the cause of the aggression). It felt counter-intuitive, but did cut through the tantrum.

Like most therapeutic parents, we became rather adept at reading the situation and adjusting the method of coming out of the dysregulation accordingly.

Another incident of note was when William took George to the local garden centre. Normally a very peaceful and empty place, but before William knew it, George had destroyed the shop, climbed on the counters and urinated on someone's car. I wasn't there, and can't pinpoint the trigger, but I imagine it had to do with saying 'no' to something George wanted at the time. It's a funny anecdote in hindsight, but scary and mortifying at the time.

We needed to do what we thought was best, no matter what people who knew us, or didn't know us, thought. Sometimes friends with birth children had very little understanding of what we were trying to do with George. Unfortunately, some of our friends just couldn't wrap their head around therapeutic parenting, and the need to approach raising a child differently, and we actually had to distance ourselves from them for a time. We knew that this wouldn't last forever, and we were dedicated to a therapeutic parenting approach; we wanted to help George NOW, so we could move forward, not simply scare him into submission until it all exploded later. Yes, it was unconventional.

Tricky situations

School was a tricky situation. There were a few examples, speckled across nursery and reception, of George punching and kicking with varying degrees of severity. Most of them seemed to be related to George's ongoing difficulty with understanding his own strength, and what we would come to call dyspraxia. The worst case of all was at a soft play centre. George had some sort of falling out with a girl of similar age. He put his hands around her neck, causing her to have an asthma attack and to need her inhaler. Luckily her mother owned the centre and was on hand. After much apologising and explaining, she calmed down and said she understood, though we didn't go back there for a long time!

It was much easier to deal with situations at home of course, with fewer variables, and mostly no other people around. There were, however, a few very tricky situations, and moments when we got it all totally wrong.

Once, we had a rather exciting day planned. In the evening we (William and I) were set to go to a birthday dinner, whist a babysitter stayed with George. William thought it would be a good idea to do some errands and have a fun afternoon with George beforehand. Into the bookstore they went, in search of a present. Action: meltdown number 1. Into the card shop (meltdown 2), then to the cinema. Although they'd had popcorn during the film, on the way out, seeing the ice creams, George had such a volcanic explosion that people were gathered around as William tried to contain and calm him. It got so bad that William had to call me to come to the cinema, and between the two of us we managed to get George home. This was one time when we had to explain the situation to strangers who had gathered, as they presumed we were trying to kidnap our own son! Unfortunately, George was far too dysregulated to allow us to carry on with our own plans. We had to cancel the babysitter and stay home as a family. There was a lot of that in those days…

Another unavoidable situation arose nine months into the adoption. My sister was getting married in the US at Disney World. It almost doesn't bear discussing, as all of the triggers were rolled into one: a continual string of snacks and distractions on the plane with an over-excited and tired four-year-old. Once there, George was constantly running away, eating rubbish food, which led to public temper tantrums and meltdowns, several instances of physical aggression, an exhausted family and a rather strained family relationship.

With our adoptive parent crystal ball, we tried to look beyond George's behaviours to what may have happened in the first two-and-a-half years of his life. Frequently, when we'd said 'no' to something, or tried to divert him from what he wanted, George would throw a tantrum. And sometimes, when we still weren't going along with his "wants", George would attempt to choke us. Is this something he'd seen done in his early life, when a parent was angry, or not getting what they wanted?

When a situation like that arose, we would have to stay as calm as possible. In our own birth families, we would have had a "time out" or have to sit on the naughty step, to "think about what we'd done". Our support workers and the GBB encouraged us to never do "time out", only "time in". For an adopted child, especially one who has experienced neglect early in life, time out means being pushed away, teaching them that they are un-loveable. Time out would equal neglect for George and result in another disaster (the few times we tried it). Instead, we learned to wait until we could compose ourselves, then sit down and talk about what had happened, and calmly explain the reasons for saying 'no'. It was challenging, but we were slowly re-programming George's brain towards self-regulation.

Telling the story

As modern adoptive parents, we all walk a bit of a tightrope when it comes to talking about our child's birth family. We wanted George to think of his birth mother, Dani, in a positive light – important for his emotional state now and in the future. 'Dani loves you very much' and 'Dani tried her best' were a few of the lines we used. Obviously, because George was four years old when we met, there was no way of avoiding his past, nor would we want him to. Also, it goes without saying, that as two male adopters, we didn't have much of a choice – it wouldn't be long before George realised the biological implications of being a child with two fathers! We were so grateful to the post-adoptive therapy team, who helped us all to reconcile George's past with his current behaviour.

Inevitably, the time came when George said, 'If Dani loves me so much, why can't I go back to her, or see her again?' Heart-breaking, and frankly, we didn't know how to answer that question truthfully and appropriately. Luckily, this is a very common situation, and help was at hand. We were advised that it was time to do more life story work with George. George was six-and-a-half years old, the adoption had been finalised, and we'd been together as a family for two-and-a-half years at this point.

As George couldn't read at this time, the post-adoption

SECTION 11

team created a gigantic visual timeline of George's early years. They had gone through George's extensive records, and marked all of the moves little George had experienced before he came to us (lots). There were birthday cakes to mark the years, and houses to mark the moves. Most importantly and to the point, there were police cars to mark the known instances when police had visited Dani and little George. There were 14 police cars. A total of 14 situations so bad that police had to be called, or that they had called on Dani and George because the social workers didn't feel safe to visit.

Little six-and-a-half-year-old George stared at the timeline in front of him. There was the time he moved to his biological grandmother's home until she decided she couldn't keep him. There was a time they moved to a friend's house...then another friend's, then another. There were the police cars, sandwiched between birthday cakes. No more police cars after the move to the foster family. Unfortunately, there was the fire at the foster family's home, and another move to temporary accommodation, then back to the foster home. There was our home, the final move, and then up to this point, with a few birthday cakes in between.

George looked and looked, totally still and totally silent. Then he looked up at us, with those beautiful, soul-filled eyes and said, 'Why did they leave me there so long, if I wasn't safe?'

Even now, I'm crying as I write this. Why indeed? I had to guard myself from anger and frustration and respond in the most helpful way possible.

We explained that Dani tried as best as she could, but it really wasn't enough to keep George safe, and so eventually a judge (depicted as a wise owl on the timeline) decided that it was time to make sure little George had a "forever home" where he could always be safe and looked after.

In my opinion, this was the saddest but also the most important moment since we'd become a family, and marked a turning point in our relationship. Whatever strings of attachment that bound George to Dani, holding him back from true attachment to us, fell away.

Not only did our attachments grow from that point, but there was a marked and steady decline in physical aggression, both towards us and others.

That summer, we relocated from our flat in the city to the countryside. We were very careful to make the move as gentle as possible, and stressed that it was the best thing for all of us, as a family. Our jobs were more or less mobile, and it seemed sensible. Whenever we'd visited the countryside, we'd seen a totally different George – happy and carefree, wild and safe. It was a no-brainer for us, and I like to think that none of us look back.

And now

It has been years since George lashed out physically, and in fact, I can't remember the last time he hit anyone, even in what could be called a "boyish tussle". There are still very rare moments when George will respond to a situation more aggressively than his peers, and that is generally when he feels there has been a great

SECTION II

injustice and feels unsafe. Luckily, the school he's at now is incredibly thoughtful and supportive and he recovers quickly from these situations.

Six years in, we have a healthy, happy child who is secure in his attachment to us. Thanks to our open communication and his work with our therapy team, every teacher George has remarks on his emotional intelligence and ability to communicate how he feels.

It is hard to imagine that this boy, proudly holding up a drawing and asking my opinion, is the same one who would kick and hit and bite when he didn't get what he wanted. It is hard to imagine that I am the same person who had to carry cheese for snacks in every pocket and warn friends and schools ahead of time that our son was prone to lashing out physically, and having to suggest how they might deal with it.

No, it wasn't always like this.

But we always hoped we would get to this point, this place of peace was always the goal, "do the work now for a better future", even when things were difficult.

And doesn't that feel good.

References

Brennan I et al (2022) *Comprehensive Needs Assessment of Child/Adolescent to Parent Violence and Abuse in London: Final report*, London: Mayor of London Violence Reduction Unit, available at: https://bit.ly/3LmHIYf

Condry R and Miles C (2014) 'Adolescent to parent violence: framing and mapping a hidden problem', *Criminology & Criminal Justice*, 14:3, pp.257–275

Fenton K with Johnson E (2019) *Parenting a Child with Toileting Issues*, London: CoramBAAF

Fisher S (2017) *Connective Parenting: A guide to connecting with your child using the NVR approach*, self-published

Gallagher E (2008) *Children's Violence to Parents: A critical literature review*, Master's thesis, Monash University

Hartling L, Rosen W, Walker M and Jordan J (2000) *Shame and Humiliation: From isolation to relational transformation*, Wellesley, MA: Wellesley Centers for Women

Herman J (2022) *Trauma and Recovery. From domestic abuse to political terror*, London: Pandora

Hughes D (2007) *Attachment-Focussed Family Therapy*, New York, NY: Norton & Co

Hughes D (2017) 'Dyadic Developmental Psychotherapy (DDP): an attachment-focused family treatment for developmental trauma', *Australian and New Zealand Journal of Family Therapy*, 38:4, pp.595–605

Janoff-Bulman R (1992) *Shattered Assumptions: Towards a new psychology of trauma*, New York, NY: Free Press

Lloyd S (2020) *Building Sensorimotor Systems in Children with Developmental Trauma. A model for practice*, London: Jessica Kingsley Publishers

Paterson R, Luntz H, Perlesz A and Cotton S (2002) 'Adolescent violence towards parents: maintaining family connections when the going gets tough', *Australian and New Zealand Journal of Family Therapy*, 23:2, pp.90–100

Reid VM, Dunn K, Young RJ, Amu J, Donovan T and Reissland N (2017) 'The human fetus preferentially engages with face-like visual stimuli', *Current Biology*, 27:13, pp.1825–1828

Selwyn J, Wijedasa D and Meakings S (2015) *Beyond the Adoption Order: Challenges, interventions and adoption disruption*, London: BAAF

Siegel DJ and Payne Bryson T (2011) *The Whole Brain Child: 12 proven strategies to nurture your child's developing mind*, London: Bantam Book

Tew J and Nixon J (2010) 'Parent abuse: opening up a discussion of a complex instance of family power relations', *Social Policy and Society*, 9:4, pp.579–589

Thorley W and Coates A (2017) *Child–Parent Violence (CPV): An exploratory exercise*, discussion paper, Sunderland: University of Sunderland, available at: https://sure.sunderland.ac.uk/id/eprint/6896/

van der Kolk B (2014) *The Body Keeps the Score: Mind, brain and body in the transformation of trauma*, London: Penguin Random House

113

Glossary

Adoption Support Fund – provides funds to local authorities and regional adoption agencies (RAAs) in England to pay for essential therapeutic services for eligible adoptive and special guardianship order (SGO) families. The charity Adoption in Scotland provides information on how to access similar support in Scotland. Information about adoption support services in Northern Ireland is provided by HSC NI Adoption and Foster Care. Families in Wales can access this information through the National Adoption Service.

Dysregulation – emotional dysregulation refers to an inability to control emotional states and moods.

Modelling – children watch and learn from their parents' and carers' behaviour. Modelling is intentionally behaving in a certain way to enable children to learn specific skills.

Non-Violent Resistance (NVR) – Non-Violent Resistance aims to help parents and carers address violent and destructive behaviour in children and adolescents using strategies inspired by Mahatma Gandhi, Martin Luther King and Rosa Parks. More information can be found at: www.nonviolentresistance.org.uk.

Nurture – refers to parenting and caring activities that are aimed at creating and strengthening the emotional bond with the child and to strengthen family relationships.

Post-Traumatic Stress Disorder (PTSD) – a mental health disorder that is triggered by witnessing or experiencing terrifying or life-threatening situations. Symptoms may include flashbacks, nightmares and severe anxiety, as well as intrusive thoughts.

Proprioceptive system – part of the sensory system, the proprioceptive system lets us know what our body is doing and where our limbs are in space. A smooth-running proprioceptive system helps us to know how much pressure or force to use when picking up a cup, or closing a door.

Secondary trauma – the emotional impact of trying to support someone who has experienced trauma. Symptoms of secondary trauma could include tiredness, cynicism, hopelessness, re-experiencing traumatic events, sadness and anger.

Sensory processing – refers to the way in which the brain receives, organises and responds to information from the senses. The sensory system helps us to react to, and interact with, our environment.

Shame resilience – the capacity to recognise the impact of shame and what triggers feelings of shame. Elements of shame resilience are an ability to ask for support and talk about shame with trusted others. More information can be found at: https://brenebrown.com/the-research/.

Survival response – this response is our body's reaction to danger and helps us to survive stressful and life-threatening situations. The response is triggered by a release of hormones into the body to prepare us to fight, run away or freeze.

Tactile system – our sense of touch, part of the sensory system.

Theraplay – this form of therapy supports children and their parents or carers through attachment- and play-based games and activities aimed at strengthening the relationship between them. More information can be found at: https://www.wp.theraplay.org/uk/.

Toxic shame – an intense feeling of worthlessness and physical symptoms such as raised heartbeat, change in temperature and tingling feelings.

Vestibular system – part of the sensory system. When working smoothly, the vestibular system provides a sense of balance and stability when sitting, lying down or moving around.

Useful organisations

BUSS (Building Underdeveloped Sensory Systems)

Service offering sensory-focused interventions for children who have experienced abuse and neglect and their families.

Unit 28(1), Springfield Mills
Bagley Lane, Farsley
Leeds LS28 5LY
Email: info@BUSSmodel.org
Tel: 01423 276203
https://bussmodel.org/

Centre for Adoption Support

A support and therapy service supporting adoption and permanency in the North West of England, Yorkshire and North Wales, delivered by the voluntary adoption agency Adoption Matters.

Unit 412b Chadwick House
Birchwood Park
Warrington WA3 6AE
Email: info@centreforadoptionsupport.org
Tel: 01925 982 243
www.adoptionmatters.org/cfas/

Coram Post-Adoption Support

An agency offering post-adoption support to adoptive
families.
41 Brunswick Square
London WC1N 1AZ
Email: post-adoptionservice@coram.org.uk
Tel: 020 7520 0332
www.coram.org.uk

Family Futures

An adoption agency and fostering provider; also an
assessment and treatment service for traumatised children.
440a Hornsey Road
London N19 4EB
Email: contact@familyfutures.co.uk
Tel: 020 7354 4161
www.familyfutures.co.uk

PAC-UK

An adoption support agency with offices in London, Leeds
and Liverpool. Provides individualised support for families
and children, parent groups and workshops.
Head Office
34 Wharf Road
London N1 7GR
Tel: 020 7284 0555
Advice Line: 020 7284 5879
www.pac-uk.org